Churches and Chapels of the South Downs National Park

by David Parsons
and
Robin Milner-Gulland

ISBN 978-0-904973-27-3

Published by the Sussex Archaeological Society, Lewes

Printed in Great Britain by Short Run Press, Exeter

Note on Authorship and Abbreviations

The text has been written by David Parsons (DP) unless otherwise stated, the remainder by Robin Milner-Gulland (RM-G) or jointly. The authors have exchanged drafts throughout the writing process; each has contributed to the other's pieces and they take joint responsibility for the final text. Photographs are © David Parsons unless otherwise attributed. The local authority areas in the South Downs National Park (SDNP) are the eastern part of Hampshire (H), West Sussex (WSx) and East Sussex (ESx). N, S, E, W refer to north, south, east west respectively. Sts is short for saints and RC means Roman Catholic.

Contents

Churches and Chapels of the South Downs National Park

Introduction
(RM-G with DP)

Among the tens of thousands of churches and chapels that punctuate and give particular meaning to the English land-scape, those of the South Downs are, we believe, a distinctive group, and hold a special place in the affections of those who know and specially value them. The nature of this distinctiveness derives, as one might expect, both from history and geography. To generalize: the Downland churches are typically small; they are thickly-clustered, particularly along the spring-line along the foot of the northern escarpment; they are picturesque, rustic, no two alike; they are old – at core usually 11th- or 12th-century; they are unostentatious (there is no equivalent of the imposing, finely-crafted late medieval church architecture encountered in say East Anglia). They make inventive use of the varied but mostly inadequate building materials the Downland area could supply or that could be imported without too great expense – more on this subject below. They are full of fascinating, but again unostentatious details: plenty of carving, but no grand sculptural schemes, and little surviving stained glass. In compensation the area contains several remarkable, and remarkably early, examples of that most evocative of vernacular medieval art forms, wall paintings.

The South Downs area seems to have been rather prosperous and populous in Roman and Anglo-Saxon times: there were good conditions for mixed agriculture and particularly grain-growing, with a useful string of ports giving access to the Continent (and several sturdy castles for defence). A glance at the parish system, in the process of formation in the late Anglo-Saxon period, shows settlements worthy of a church every mile or so along the spring-line already mentioned – these

Sullington, St Mary from SE, showing a simple nave and chancel church with a low west tower

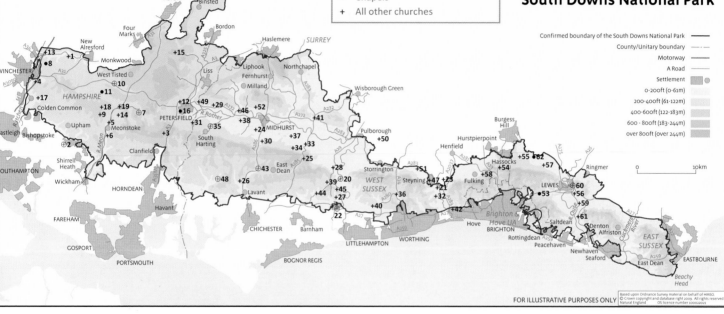

The location of churches in 1086, as recorded in Domesday Book. Many of these will have been in existence since before the Norman Conquest. The east end of the Park is a blank because churches were not recorded in the area immediately east of South Malling (Pevensey Rape), so that known early minsters, such as Beddingham and Bishopstone, do not figure on the map.

defra
Department for Environment
Food and Rural Affairs

NATURAL ENGLAND

South Downs National Park

⊕ 'Superior' or minster churches
● Chapels
+ All other churches

Confirmed boundary of the South Downs National Park
County/Unitary boundary
Motorway
A Road
Settlement

0-200ft (0-61m)
200-400ft (61-122m)
400-600ft (122-183m)
600 - 800ft (183-244m)
over 800ft (over 244m)

0   10km

FOR ILLUSTRATIVE PURPOSES ONLY

Based upon Ordnance Survey material on behalf of HMSO.
© Crown copyright and database right 2009. All rights reserved
Natural England   OS licence number 100022021

Hampshire
1. Avington
2. Bishop's Waltham
3. Chalton (churches: number not known
4. Chilcomb – 9 churches!
5. Corhampton
6. Droxford
7. East Meon
8. Easton (2 chapels)
9. Exton
10. Hinton Ampner
11. Kilmeston (chapel)
12. Mapledurham

13. Martyr Worthy
14. Meonstoke
15. Newton Vallance
16. Sunwood (chapel)
17. Twyford
18. Warnford
19. West Meon

West Sussex
20. Amberley
21. Annington/Botolphs
22. Arundel
23. Beeding (Bramber) – 2 churches

24. Bepton
25. Bignor
26. Binderton
27. Burpham
28. Bury (Arundel)
29. Chithurst
30. Cocking
31. Compton
32. Coombes
33. Duncton
34. East Lavington
35. Elsted
36. Findon
37. Graffham

38. Linch
39. North Stoke
40. Patching
41. Petworth
42. Shoreham
43. Singleton
44. Slindon
45. South Stoke
46. Stedham
47. Steyning – 2 churches
48. Stoughton
49. Trotton
50. West Chiltington
51. Wiston

52. Woolbeding

East Sussex (pre-1974)
53. Balmer (chapel)
54. Clayton
55. Ditchling
56. Iford
57. Plumpton
58. Poynings
59. Rodmell
60. South Malling
61. Southease
62. Streat (2 chapels)

parishes were characteristically elongated along a north-south axis, to give each a section of different landscape types from the wooded clay, through productive arable land to the grassy chalk hills. Often they had their own swine-pastures deep in the Weald (which might later become settlements needing their own chapels). Later in the Middle Ages, however, the area ceased to share in the general expansion of English prosperity. The ports began to silt up; there were no new resources to be exploited (the famous Wealden iron industry flourished far away from the Downs); links with the rest of the country were poor; there were few great estates to generate extra work opportunities. In the late Middle Ages and early modern period churches might be repaired or expanded, but few were built. Things changed in the 19th century, when even village churches frequently underwent restoration, and in the more urbanized areas new churches and nonconformist chapels appeared. But the heavy hand of Victorian restoration and rebuilding was felt, perhaps, more lightly in the Downland villages than elsewhere, no doubt often through lack of funds, to the benefit of early features that survived.

This book is an attempt to present this heritage to the interested non-specialist reader. With well over 200 places of worship, each of them in its own way significant, in the South Downs, it cannot be a comprehensive guide. For that purpose only the relevant volumes of Pevsner's 'Buildings of England' series can serve. To keep this volume within reasonable limits, and (we hope) to treat the material in a new and engaging way, the authors have decided to start with a series of short essays on aspects of the church heritage, its significance in its location, the history and nature of its main features; then to continue with a more detailed study of some 50 buildings of particular interest. Our geographical limits are set by the boundary of the South Downs National Park. This includes not just the chalkland itself (where settlements have historically been rather sparse), but most importantly the contiguous villages beneath the northern (in East Hampshire, eastern) scarp; also a considerable area of West Sussex, reaching to the Surrey border, often known as the 'Western Weald'. In this part the geology differs somewhat from elsewhere in the SDNP, and somewhat different building materials are normal – but as it happens it contains

rather fewer villages with churches selected for this publication. The SDNP includes a series of market towns, whose churches naturally tend to be larger than those of the villages, but do not materially affect the points we make. What the National Park (importantly) excludes are the larger conurbations nearby, as well as the coastal plain generally. It so happens that the latter – unlike the Downland proper – contains several large, important and rather ornate Romanesque and later churches. There are others on the northern edge of the Park, such as Petworth (WSx) – off the Downs, but actually within SDNP – and Arundel (WSx) on the south, where the late medieval parish church stands on the north side of London Road, while the important 19th-century Roman Catholic cathedral is on the south side, just outside the Park: the boundary here runs along the middle of the road. This sort of complication arises from the fact that the SDNP boundary is a negotiated line, and does not always coincide with established boundaries, whether natural or man-made. Again in West Sussex, the area around Steyning is potentially problematic: part of Steyning parish is in SDNP, but its historically highly important church is not – we would hardly be justified in omitting it.

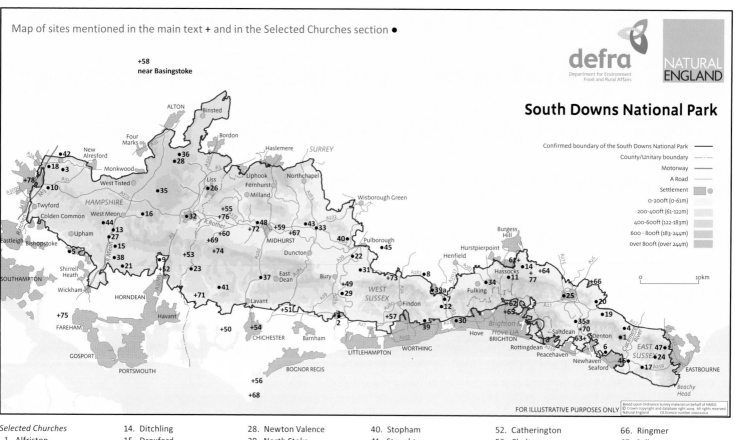

Map of sites mentioned in the main text + and in the Selected Churches section ●

South Downs National Park

Confirmed boundary of the South Downs National Park —
County/Unitary boundary — · —
Motorway —
A Road —
Settlement ▢ ●
0-200ft (0-61m)
200-400ft (61-122m)
400-600ft (122-183m)
600 - 800ft (183-244m)
over 800ft (over 244m)

0   10km

FOR ILLUSTRATIVE PURPOSES ONLY

Based upon Ordnance Survey material on behalf of HMSO.
© Crown copyright and database right 2009. All rights reserved.
Natural England   OS licence number 100022021

Selected Churches
1. Alfriston
2. Arundel
3. Avington
4. Berwick
5. Bishop's Waltham
6. Bishopstone
7. Botolphs
8. Buncton
9. Clanfield
10. Chilcomb
11. Clayton
12. Coombes
13. Corhampton
14. Ditchling
15. Droxford
16. East Meon
17. East Dean
18. Easton
19. Firle
20. Glynde
21. Hambledon
22. Hardham & Greatham
23. Idsworth
24. Jevington
25. Lewes
26. Liss
27. Meonstoke
28. Newton Valence
29. North Stoke
30. Old Shoreham
31. Parham
32. Petersfield
33. Petworth
34. Poynings
35. Privett
35a. Rodmell
36. Selborne
37. Singleton
38. Soberton
39. Sompting
39a. Steyning
40. Stopham
41. Stoughton
42. The Itchens
43. Tillington
44. Warnford
45. West Chiltington
46. Westdean
47. Willingdon
48. Woolbeding

Main text
49. Amberley
50. Bosham
51. Boxgrove
52. Catherington
53. Chalton
54. Chichester
55. Chithurst
56. Church Norton
57. Clapham
58. Cowdery's Down
59. Easebourne
60. Elsted
61. Keymer
62. Patcham
63. Piddinghoe
64. Plumpton
65. Preston
66. Ringmer
67. Selham
68. Selsey
69. South Harting
70. Southease
71. Stansted
72. Stedham
73. Sullington
74. The Mardens
75. Titchfield
76. Trotton
77. Westmeston
78. Winchester

The neighbouring parish of Wiston contains two medieval churches, of which one – the more interesting – lies just outside, the other just inside, the actual Park boundary. We have decided to include the 'outsiders' and hope that such decisions will seem justified to our readers.

Thus we have included Steyning as the sole example in the area of a grand Romanesque basilica, and the nearby Buncton, a humble church that surprisingly incorporates bits of very high quality carved stonework, obviously brought from elsewhere. As noted above, Arundel Cathedral is included since it is an important example of Victorian architecture and because it is one of very few Roman Catholic places of worship in or near the Park; Old Shoreham as much for its location at the river crossing of an ancient routeway (beside which Sompting – inside the Park boundary – also stands) as for its historical importance;

and West Chiltington because its later medieval wall paintings make points of comparison and contrast with the early murals at such places as Hardham and Clayton. The potential corpus of churches worth visiting is thereby considerably enhanced, particularly in West Sussex, where already there was an *embarras de richesses*. Because of limitations of space other almost equally worthy candidates have had to be left out, for example the delightful Mardens high up in the hills and thought by many to be archetypical Downland churches; or Selham, with its intriguing carved capitals and herringbone masonry; or Elsted with its fabric evidence for deconstruction and reconstruction. But though they do not figure among the *Selected Churches* we have tried to make mention of them at appropriate points in the thematic 'essays' that follow. In East Sussex and Hampshire the problem is less acute, though the number of interesting

places of worship in Lewes, the county town, tends to overbalance the East Sussex corpus; we have added Alfriston to the original list to the exclusion of Beddingham, notwithstanding the latter's importance as an early centre of Christianity. In Hampshire Bishop's Waltham has been included instead of Chalton, which historically is of almost equal importance.

We have tried to achieve a balance: geographically by the proportions of the three constituent parts of the Park – Hampshire and West Sussex roughly two fifths each, East Sussex one fifth – by architectural period, by historical importance and by the 'extras' of special interest, such as furniture and monuments. The accompanying map shows the places of worship mentioned either in the *Selected Churches* section or in these introductory essays.

What is a church?

The word 'church', or at least its Latin and Greek equivalents, originally meant a community of adherents to the Christian religion. At first there were no purpose-built places of worship, and congregations met in rooms set aside in members' private houses, as at Lullingstone Roman villa in Kent, where a room was painted out with figures of people at prayer and the Christian *chi-rho* symbol. By the time Christianity was introduced into Anglo-Saxon England some centuries later it was normal to have specialist buildings set aside for worship, and some of the early churches were old Roman buildings reused. But as the religion took hold, more worship centres had to be built from scratch, though in some cases on top of earlier buildings; in Sussex the church excavated at Bargham, in Angmering parish, seemed possibly to overlie a Roman building. The simplest form was a plain rectangular room; hardly any churches of this form survive, since most were rebuilt or added to over the centuries, but there is a rare

North Marden, St Mary, from SE

example of a single-celled church in SDNP at Greatham (WSx), where the east wall still shows evidence of its original single small window. The date of this church is probably late 11th-century. A little later – 12th-century – is North Marden (WSx), a slightly more developed form with a rounded east end, or apse, which has three windows.

Early on the influence of native house-building traditions can be seen. In the first place the basic building material was timber, and there is considerable historical and archaeological evidence for wooden churches, most of which were replaced

Greatham church from SE

Idsworth, St Hubert, from SW

Chilcomb, St Andrew, from S

in stone in the course of the Middle Ages. Because of the perishable nature of their building materials, substantial Anglo-Saxon houses, great halls, even some palaces, many of which are known archaeologically, have not survived above ground. Nationally important examples have been excavated locally, notably at Chalton (H) and Bishopstone (ESx) in the area of the Park, and at Cowdery's Down, near Basingstoke (H), a dozen miles north-east of the most northerly point in the Park. Typically these houses consisted of a large rectangular room, with a narrower square annex at one or both ends. They

seem to have suggested the form of the earliest churches, which had rectangular naves with narrower chambers (chancels) at the east end. Though this basic structure was often extended by the addition of side chambers (aisles or transepts) and towers, there are still examples of simple nave-and-chancel churches to be found, e.g. at Chilcomb and Idsworth (H).

Another aspect of the relationship between churches and domestic buildings may be mentioned here. Places of worship of all kinds, from the great minsters and monasteries such as Westminster to the

smallest churches and chapels, were typically founded by landowners, from the king down to the lords of the most insignificant manors. They were founded on private property and remained the landowners' possessions; they could be bought, sold, given away or exchanged, or even reclaimed from the Church – a scandal that the Venerable Bede was complaining about as early as the beginning of the 8th century. It follows that the siting of places of worship was determined by the location of the founders' property. In the case of the major minsters, the early centres of Christian mission and subsequent pastoral care, a close correlation has been demonstrated in some areas between royal and episcopal (i.e. bishops') estate centres and the sites of the minsters themselves; Hampshire is one such area. At manorial level the parish church is often to be found cheek by jowl with the manor house, and looks much as though it might be a private chapel rather than a place for public worship. The two can be indistinguishable where the 'public' were none other than the staff of the house and the estate workers. There are good examples of this phenomenon in the area of SDNP.

Botolphs, St Botolph, from NW, showing blocked N arcade

examples at Parham, Woolbeding and Stansted, and in East Sussex at Glynde and Firle. Hampshire examples include Newton Vallence and Warnford, where the ruins of the medieval manor house still stand to the east of the church. At Bishop's Waltham the church is the successor to the Anglo-Saxon minster of an episcopal estate, as the place-name implies.

By the end of the Middle Ages, however, most churches and many chapels had developed more complex forms, and unravelling their structural history is one of the rewarding things about church visiting (see below the section on Clues, p. 23).

The present public entrance to Petworth House (WSx) is through a door adjacent to the south churchyard wall, and the churchyard itself is bounded to west and north by the park wall. At Arundel (WSx) the church is adjacent to the castle; its chancel, after many long-running disputes, is still the prerogative of the Dukes of Norfolk, who remain Roman Catholic, and is accessible only from the castle. A screen (currently of glass) separates it from the body of the church. There could hardly be a better illustration of the seigneurial aspects of the parish church. Elsewhere in West Sussex there are more 'downmarket'

Avington, St Mary, from SE, showing nave and W tower

This kind of development virtually ceased at the Reformation. By about 1550 the worship of the recently established Anglican Church had been drastically simplified, and in due course many of their buildings were reduced to match: for example, side aisles were often removed, leaving tell-tale ranges of blocked arches which had formerly connected them to the body of the church, as at Botolphs (WSx).

Glynde St Mary from SW, showing nave, W porch and bell turret

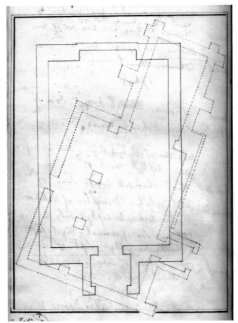

Glynde St Mary, extract from parish register 1765 (ESRO PAR 347-1-1-1, p. 98)

New buildings, which were rarely required, were planned on more straightforward lines: there are examples in SDNP from the 18th century, at Avington (H) and Glynde (ESx, see p. 124), both single-celled buildings, though Avington also has a west tower.

At the same time new sects were growing up (Sussex in particular was a hotbed of Dissent) and needed alternative places of worship. Many of these were converted domestic buildings, and those that were newly built often adopted the same architectural style, for instance at Ditchling (ESx).

These were sometimes known as chapels, sometimes as meeting houses, though gradually the word 'church' was also used in some Nonconformist circles. By the 19th century more formal architectural forms were also reintroduced, initially the neo-Classical style represented by Avington and Glynde, but later the neo-Gothic which was popular in Victorian church-building by the Church of England (the Baptists were among the latest to be 'converted' to this).

Ditchling Old Meeting House, with tile-hung cottage attached on its left

Christianity in East Hampshire and Sussex

It is well known that Christianity was introduced into this country during the Roman period (e.g. the Lullingstone villa mentioned above), but it is less clear how widespread and effective it was among the civil population. The organization of the early Church was based on the major towns, which declined once the Roman administration withdrew from the provinces of Britain around AD400. Most parts of England were then settled by groups of Germanic people, known collectively as Anglo-Saxons, who still adhered to their traditional religion, as place-names such as Patchway (in SDNP at Stanmer Park between Brighton and Lewes), which refers to a heathen sanctuary, testify. More obviously related to the names of pagan gods – in this case Thor/Thunor – are *Thunorslege* (ESx, beyond the Park near Bexhill) and *Thunreslea* (H, in the Meon Valley), both 'lost' names attested in ancient documents. How far Romano-British

Christianity survived under pagan rule is not known, but the new Anglo-Saxon élite stood in need of conversion. This was achieved by St Augustine's mission to Kent at the end of the 6th century and by a parallel mission in the north-east on the part of monks from Ireland.

The progress of the conversion was uncertain and had to be carried out through the local rulers of the kingdoms and tribal areas which now controlled much of England. A pattern developed whereby kings of still pagan kingdoms married the daughters of kings who were already Christian, adopting the new religion as a consequence and often as a condition of the marriage. This procedure was followed in the late 7th century in the territory which forms much of the present National Park. The then king of the South Saxons (i.e. Sussex), named Æthelwalh, married a Christian princess from the south-west midlands, and the powerful king of west midland Mercia, as his overlord, sponsored him as a candidate for baptism. He further endowed him with territory in the Meon Valley and the Isle of

Church Norton: the surviving chancel of the medieval church; the rest was removed to Selsey in the 19th century

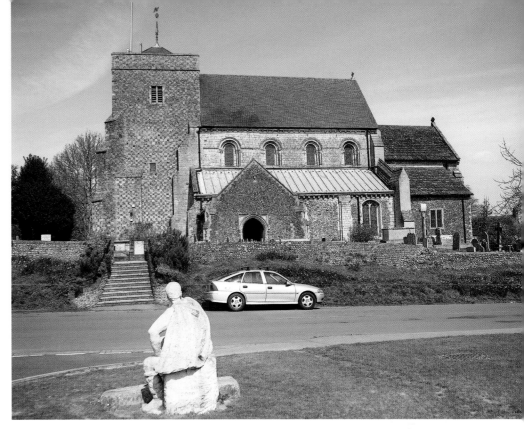

Wight; this may simply have confirmed an earlier political entity, which it is thought was in existence in the Roman period and administered from the local tribal capital, Chichester.

At this juncture the future saint Wilfrid appeared on the scene. He was already a bishop, nominally of York, but in exile from his see for political and personal reasons. According to the Venerable Bede, whose *Ecclesiastical History* was written within half a century of these events, Wilfrid found a small community of Irish monks in the Bosham area, whose missionary attempts, if any, had fallen on deaf ears. He set about rectifying this, and the king granted him a substantial estate on the Selsey peninsula on which to establish his mission. Its centre appears to have been not the modern town of Selsey itself, but Church Norton, where the chancel of the later medieval church still survives.

The Christianization and subsequent pastoral care of the population were carried out from similar estate centres throughout Sussex and the Meon Valley, which were similarly donated by royalty and aristocratic families and recorded in charters (the Anglo-Saxon equivalent of conveyances). The more northerly parts of East Hampshire were under the aegis of the longer-established bishopric of Winchester. The aristocratic founders of what were effectively regional churches known as minsters (individual parishes were not to develop until a few centuries later) sometimes came to be regarded as local saints. A case in point in the Park area is the legend of the foundation of Steyning church (WSx) by St Cuthman, the 'boy with a cart', supposedly a shepherd who pushed his invalid mother across country in a 'wheelbarrow' from the Chidham area until they reached Steyning, where the carrying strap broke and was interpreted as a divine indication of the place to build a minster church.

In reality, the saintly founder is likely to have been of high social status (Cuth– is an aristocratic name element), and the wheelbarrow a litter in which a high-born lady might travel. The very impressive and ornate Romanesque church built on the site after the Norman Conquest bears out the high status of the original minster and its founder. Elsewhere in the National Park, at Bishopstone (ESx), there is another saint's legend, in which a cleric from the Low Countries attempted in the 11th century to steal the relics of St Lewinna (of whom nothing else is known).

These early estates tended to become subdivided as parts were sold off, exchanged, or given away as a reward for services. In their turn the owners or tenants of these smaller landholdings founded and financed churches on their own property for their own convenience and for the use of their estate workers. It is this proliferation of local churches that led to the establishment of the parish system.

The number of churches in existence by the time of the Domesday Survey (1086) shows the extent of this development by the end of the 11th century (see map above, p. 2), but it continued at least for another century. Even then there were settlements which did not have their own independent parish church until much later. A good example in the area of the Park is Petersfield (H), where the church, despite its size and grandeur, was a mere chapel dependent on the mother church at Buriton until 1886.

By around 1200 further changes were taking place in both parish churches and parochial chapels. The veneration of the saints, particularly the Blessed Virgin Mary, which had been a feature of the Anglo-Saxon church, now found architectural expression as the concept of Purgatory took hold in the Western (i.e. Roman Catholic) Church and people sought the intercession of the saints on their behalf. The need to accommodate altars dedicated to St Mary and other saints led to the addition of transepts, side aisles and chapels, which in many cases totally altered the shape of the original building. Many of these – and in some cases separate chapels erected in the churchyard

– will have attracted chantry foundations, that is the endowment of landed property to employ a priest or priests to say Masses at specified intervals on behalf of the founder and his/her family. The founder could be a group, such as a craft guild, in which case the Masses would benefit all members of the group. For individuals who were not members of such guilds or of religious fraternities there were private devotions at the altar of a saint. The saints were expected to intervene on behalf of their devotees not only for their spiritual well-being but also to protect them from the hazards of everyday life, such as childbirth. The notion of St Christopher safeguarding travellers has persisted into modern secular times.

Another development in the later Middle Ages was the emphasis on the mystery of the Mass and the special status of the clergy who celebrated it. This led to chancels being lengthened or totally rebuilt, so that the main altar would be in a remote place below the east window, and to the insertion of elaborate screens between the chancel and the body of the church. The immediate focus of congregational attention was thenceforth the great crucifix or rood suspended

Petersfield, St Peter, from SE

above the screen on the nave side of the chancel arch. This was served from a gallery or 'loft', to which the access was by a staircase cut through the walling at the junction of the nave and chancel.

Much of this was swept away in the wake of the Reformation. The English Church, hitherto Roman Catholic, was 'rebranded' as the Church of England, with Henry VIII and his successors as its Head, rather than the Pope. The liturgy (the conduct of the church services) was largely unaffected for the time being, but under Henry's successor, the boy king Edward VI, the Protestant party gained the ascendency, and sweeping changes were made. By about 1550 the idea of the intercession of the saints was held to be heretical and the number of altars in church was reduced to one, making many side chapels redundant. The Mass itself was deemed of lesser importance and Holy Communion was celebrated at much less frequent intervals, so chancels, too, became underused, while the new Prayer Book replaced the Roman Missal. Images of saints, and in particular the depiction of Christ's Body, were held to be sacrilegious, and the great roods were removed.

Ditchling, St Margaret, from SE, showing the SE (Abergavenny) chapel between the house gables

New uses were found for side chapels and even for chancels, a common one being the accommodation of a school, but many were allowed to deteriorate and were eventually demolished, leaving only blocked-up arches as evidence of their former existence, for example at Botolphs (WSx), where the north aisle was removed

(see illustration above, p. 9). Often this did not take place until the 18th century, and at Elsted (WSx) the north aisle survived into the 19th, as a drawing by Henry Petrie shows.

An extreme case was Steyning (WSx), where in 1578 a commission appointed by Elizabeth I reported that the east end of the church was partly ruinous and could be dispensed with and the building materials used to better effect elsewhere; the chancel, central tower and transepts were duly demolished, and shortly after 1600 a new tower was erected at the west end.

This sketchy account of the Reformation relates only to the changes which overtook church fabrics and their contents, and looks forward to the sections below on *Furnishings and Fittings* and *Monuments and Memorials*. The impact of these changes on the worshippers at the time is difficult to assess, but whatever their theological stance vis-à-vis the reformed religion the contrast between their churches before and after the event must have been stark. The walls of medieval churches had been covered by paintings, as the restored schemes at Hardham and Clayton (WSx) show; the reformers decreed

Elsted, St Paul, nave from N showing blocked arcade arches

The long chancel of St Michael's, Up Marden, from NE

that they should be whitewashed over, thus increasing the austere appearance of church interiors. The liturgy was shorn of many of its ceremonies, for example the playlet performed each Easter around the Sepulchre in the chancel. Outdoor processions on saints' days and other festivals were banned, and the banners and streamers provided by parishioners at their own expense had to be discarded. The far-reaching social, psychological and financial effects in one English parish have been explored by Professor Eamon Duffy in his book *Voices of Morebath* (2001).

Henry Petrie's drawing of Elsted church interior, *c.*1805, showing N arcade still open with a view into the N aisle (© Sussex Archaeological Society, Sharpe Collection no.125)

The plain Protestant interior of Alfriston Congregational chapel

Itchen Stoke, St Mary, a miniature version of the Sainte Chapelle

After the ultra-Protestant regime during the Commonwealth period and the reintroduction of more traditional forms of worship under the restored monarchy, the need for new church furnishings and indeed new churches began to assert itself. The growth of London prompted a parliamentary Act in the reign of Queen Anne for the provision of 52 new churches (in the event only 12 were built). By the end of the 18th century the Industrial Revolution had led to the rapid growth of manufacturing towns in the midlands and north of England, while in the south the popularity of sea bathing saw the expansion of coastal resorts such as Brighton and Eastbourne. The existing parish churches and parochial chapels were inadequate to meet the church-going needs of the new populations, and as suburbs grew they were not in the right place to do so. Following the passing of the Church Building Act in 1818 and the voting of substantial funds by Parliament, a spate of church building took place and continued through the 19th century. These developments are scarcely represented in the National Park, since they were essentially an urban phenomenon, and the towns of the coastal strip are outside the Park boundaries, as noted in the Introduction. Nevertheless there are several examples of churches built in the Victorian period as replacements for medieval buildings which were held for various reasons to be inadequate: in Lewes (ESx), St John sub Castro is a brick church built in 1839–40, with an open interior in the manner of the 'preaching boxes' of the previous two centuries and galleries on cast-iron columns, but traceried windows in a Gothic style; of the two Itchen churches (H) in the 1860s, one built unusually in a neo-Romanesque style, the other in imitation of the Gothic Sainte Chapelle in Paris; and Privett (H), 1876–78, in the fully-fledged Gothic Revival style which had become popular after the reintroduction of medieval ritual under the influence of the Oxford Movement and the Cambridge Ecclesiological Society.

These Anglican developments were to some extent a response to the growth of Nonconformity and the spread of Dissenting places of worship, untrammelled by the restrictions of the parish system and preconceived ideas of what constituted a church building. By the time of the Church Building Act the Church of England perceived that it was losing ground to the Nonconformists, who had begun to fill the vacuum in the new industrial suburbs and the coastal towns. The seeds of Dissent were already present in Protestantism, which itself was a rejection of traditional authority. The Puritans, prominent in the 17th century, in particular during the Commonwealth period, were initially still part of the Church of England (the parish church of South Malling (ESx), built in 1632 on the ruins of an earlier collegiate church, has been described as a Puritan place of worship), but by 1670 many groups had broken away to establish their own chapels and meeting houses in which they could practise their own forms of (non-Prayer Book) worship and pursue their own beliefs, such as the concept of the priesthood of all believers, and practices like adult baptism. Again, much of this activity went on in the towns – Brighton, Lewes, Horsham, Midhurst in Sussex – but a few Nonconformist places of worship can be found in rural or semi-urban areas within the Park, notably Ditchling (ESx), Petworth (WSx) and Selborne (H).

Despite episodes like the Gunpowder Plot, Roman Catholicism was to some extent tolerated and continued to be practised in the 17th and 18th centuries, led and supported by aristocratic and gentry families who adhered to the old religion, such as the Gages in East Sussex and the Howards in West Sussex. Nevertheless there were financial and social penalties, such as exclusion from public office, and persecution took place at some times and in some areas. The situation gradually improved in the late 18th century, as a number of Catholic Relief (or Emancipation) Acts were passed, beginning in 1778 and culminating in the well-known 1829 Act. As a result Roman Catholic places of worship could be openly built, and there are examples in or near the Park at Arundel (WSx; now the cathedral of the Diocese of Arundel and Brighton), Petworth (WSx) and Petersfield (H).

The Church Fabric

Clues to the building history

Despite the importance of timber as a building material in its own right and its ancillary use in the construction process for scaffolding (see the evidence in the west wall of Stoughton church (WSx) noted in the Selected Churches entry), working platforms and templates, and despite the ready availability of timber in SDNP, especially in the Wealden area of Sussex, there is little historical woodwork surviving in the churches of the area. Medieval roofs, such as those of East Anglia, are virtually absent; there are only a few post-Reformation roofs of note, and surviving internal furnishings – from screens to font covers – are few and far between. Most of what there is to see is of 19th-century or more recent date, and offers no clues to the earlier development of the church fabrics. We have to rely therefore on the evidence of the masonry itself.

The west front of
East Meon, All Saints

When it comes to studying the church fabric, there are plenty of books that tell you what a Romanesque ('Norman') door is like, how to recognize a Perpendicular window and what the elements of a Classical church look like, and so forth. What they often do not say is that individual doors and windows were often inserted into already existing walls and sometimes salvaged during a rebuilding operation and re-erected in a newer wall. So the date of a feature is not necessarily the same as the part of the building in which it is set. To understand a building – in this case a place of worship – properly, it is important to bear in mind some of the things that show how it changed over time.

The changes usually come about because the church or chapel was being adapted to accommodate a different kind of use, either in the way church services were performed or in response to changing social needs; in the last 30 or 40 years the most frequent social developments have been the addition of toilet facilities and parish meeting rooms. In common with most other areas, some churches in SDNP, including some of the examples chosen for this book, expanded sideways in the medieval period by adding aisles to otherwise plain rectangular naves. The evidence for this can usually be seen at the west end of the buildings (less frequently at the east end because of other changes at a later date), where the aisle's end wall meets the existing quoin (corner) of the original building. Here there is no bonding of the stone courses, but what is called a *straight joint* between the two areas of masonry, and the original pattern of the quoin stones is usually still apparent, as at East Meon (H).

Another example is Bishopstone (ESx), where an aisle was added to the north side of the church; here much of the quoin was dismantled, so there is only a short section of straight joint. However, one of the original windows survives in part, and the outer reveal can still be seen – inside the church from the north aisle. Once the aisle was built the window became one of a number of *redundant features*, since it could no longer admit light from the exterior; as it stands, it is quite illogical, and would never have been built if the church had been designed with aisles from the start. *Illogicalities* such as this and *inconsistencies* are a good clue to the way in which the fabric has developed. Hambledon (H) is a case in point: here the nave is made up of two sections, and the eastern section is narrower than the other. This is odd, and comes about only because the earlier chancel (typically narrower than its nave) has been retained when the later chancel was built – oddly again wider than the eastern part of the nave, as the plan displayed inside the church shows.

Another seemingly unimportant *redundant feature* is the small blocked window in the east wall of the chancel at Greatham

Bishopstone,
St Andrew, exterior
of early window seen
from N aisle

Blocked window in the E wall of
Greatham chancel

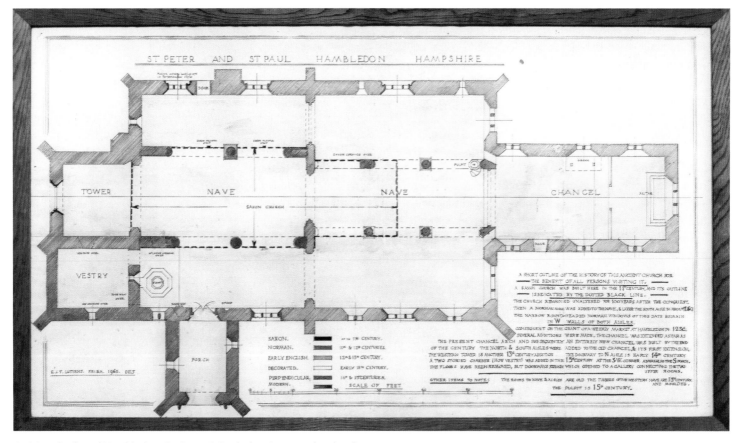

Architect's plan of Hambledon, Sts Peter & Paul, showing complex development

(WSx). This is difficult to see, but between the two lancet windows is a group of five stones, one a block carved with a curve on its underside, supported by two others to left and right with some flint infill between. This is a rare piece of evidence for a single small east window before the development in the 13th century of paired or triple lancets and long before the introduction of the big 'picture window' of multiple lights later in the Middle Ages. So this is an important observation in terms of the history of church architecture, but it also has wider implications for the way in which the chancel was used at different times and where the main altar was placed: a rather abstruse matter and not of great consequence in the context of an everyday visit, but it is an observation worth making nevertheless.

The little window at Bishopstone illustrates another point worth observing: part of it was removed when the arches of the north arcade were built: in such cases *intersecting features* often demonstrate the building sequence. It was not uncommon for medieval builders to insert doors, windows, arches and even complete arcades into existing walls. Even without the benefits of modern technology they were perfectly capable of supporting a wall while holes were made to take the masonry of the new feature, apparently without even removing the roof. The addition of aisles might make that necessary, however. Because the nave windows had become non-functional it often became desirable to add a range of windows above the original nave walls, known as a clerestory (or clearstory, which neatly indicates its purpose). The roof would then be rebuilt at a higher level, leaving a tell-tale redundant

Petersfield, St Peter, interior facing W, showing weathering of former roof

Petersfield, St Peter, S aisle and former S transept from SE

Petersfield parish church also illustrates two other diagnostic features. The south aisle wall is made up of two different fabrics: At the east end there is an area of rubble masonry which includes some stones laid in a herringbone pattern; the remainder of the walling is built of iregular stone blocks with dressed stone buttresses. The contrast is marked, and shows that the main part of the aisle was added onto an existing structure, originally the south transept. *Changes of fabric* of this sort can be recognized by differences in the shapes of the stones, as here, by differences in geological type (e.g. sandstone vs. flint), which is often signalled by changes in colour, and by the way the stones are laid (e.g. herringbone vs. horizontal courses). At Petersfield the interpretation of a two-phase fabric in the south aisle is reinforced by the second diagnostic feature: a projecting course of shaped stones (a 'moulding' or 'string course'), which runs the length of the aisle at window sill level, but stops abruptly at the buttress by the downpipe. There is no such moulding in the fabric with the herringbone courses, which is significant: linear features of this sort should continue indefinitely round a building if it is all of one build.

feature, known as a *weathering*, in the end walls below, which indicates the level and pitch of the earlier roof. The purpose of this projecting line of stones, in the shape of an inverted V, was to prevent rainwater seeping down between the roof and the end wall (at the west end often the wall of a tower). There is a good example of this at Petersfield (H; see further in the *Selected Churches* entry, also Rodmell (ESx), another complex building).

A *discontinuous feature* like this usually means that the two parts of the fabric belong to different building phases. At Hambledon (H) there is a string course at the top of the wall of the 'inner' nave, which terminates about halfway along the wall and indicates the original length of what was the chancel wall of the early church. The same sort of evidence can be provided by plinths at the base of the wall. At South Malling (ESx) there is a continuous plinth around the west tower, which returns along the west wall of the nave, implying that they are of the same build; but it does not continue around the nave of the church, which may therefore be of later date and added to an already existing wall. Alternatively, the nave may predate the tower and its own west wall. At the time of writing investigations are taking place to discover whether either of these interpretations can be proved.

Returning to Petersfield, a closer examination of the south wall of the former transept reveals another change of fabric: the masonry surrounding the lancet window is quite different in appearance and texture from the surrounding walling, and shows that the window is not an original feature, but an insertion at a later date. Here the evidence is fairly clear, but fabric changes are often quite subtle, especially where the same building material is concerned (see for instance the discussion of different kinds of flint rubble in the *Selected Churches* entry for Bishopstone, ESx).

The medieval habit of adding side aisles was reversed in many cases at or after the Reformation, when their original purpose had become obsolete. Once an aisle or side chapel was no longer required and began to need expensive maintenance, demolition might be seen as the cheaper option. A good example of a church that lost its aisle is Botolphs (WSx; see picture on p. 9). What can now be seen is the original north wall of the nave, but still with the inserted arcade which formerly led to the aisle. The redundant arches have been blocked, probably using the demolition material from the aisle walls; the blockings are of well-coursed flints, which contrast with the random flint rubble (just visible through and round the surface rendering) of the nave wall: a combination of *redundant features* and a not-too-obvious *change of fabric*. Blocked openings of this sort – doors, windows, arches – can be seen in many of the churches described in *Selected Churches*. A blocked doorway may not sound worth noting, but often indicates that the internal furnishings had been reorganized to make possible a change in the way the church was used. An example is the door in the end wall of the Old Meeting House in Ditchling (ESx), which was bricked up in 1817, and a new doorway made in the side elevation, which allowed seating to be placed against the former entrance wall. Entry was henceforth not by the main east–west lane, but by a twitten (a Sussex term for a narrow lane) at right angles to it.

End wall of Ditchling Old Meeting, with blocked original entrance door

Individually observations such as these are straightforward, and their meaning often self-evident, but when used in combination can lead to interpretations of great complexity, as for example at Petersfield (H) or Rodmell (ESx).

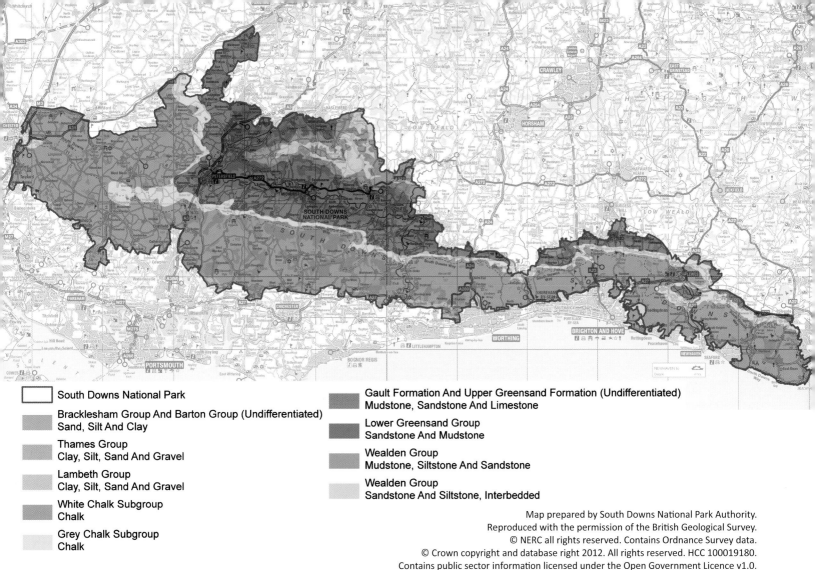

	South Downs National Park		Gault Formation And Upper Greensand Formation (Undifferentiated) Mudstone, Sandstone And Limestone
	Bracklesham Group And Barton Group (Undifferentiated) Sand, Silt And Clay		Lower Greensand Group Sandstone And Mudstone
	Thames Group Clay, Silt, Sand And Gravel		Wealden Group Mudstone, Siltstone And Sandstone
	Lambeth Group Clay, Silt, Sand And Gravel		Wealden Group Sandstone And Siltstone, Interbedded
	White Chalk Subgroup Chalk		
	Grey Chalk Subgroup Chalk		

Simplified geological map of SDNP

Building materials

From the foregoing it is clear that some knowledge of building materials, particularly stone, is helpful to the understanding of church fabrics. A useful basic guide to the local resources is David Robinson's *Geology and Scenery of the SDNP*, the third book in this series, but building stone was also drawn from outside the Park, from the Isle of Wight (Quarr, Bembridge/Binstead), and from elsewhere, including Normandy (Caen). These were relatively easily transported by water, and the river systems helped them to penetrate inland in addition to their obvious use along the coastal plain.

Local resources

The principal geological formation of the South Downs is chalk, which is not normally regarded as a building stone, because it is relatively soft and rapidly eroded by the weather if used externally. Occasionally harder varieties have been used externally for farm buildings and more often internally for detailed work in churches, such as window reveals and arch mouldings in North Stoke church (WSx). Most often, however, it was used for

Tower of Steyning parish church from SW, showing chequer-board masonry pattern

burning to quicklime, the active ingredient of lime mortar.

The Downland chalk also contains flints in large quantities, and they are used in buildings of all types as the basis for rubble walling. Flint occurs in nodules of fairly

small size, and is not suitable for dressings (quoins, window and door surrounds) or decorative work, except when used in square areas alternating with square blocks of sandstone or limestone to form a chequer pattern, as in the tower of Steyning church (WSx).

The nodules are often used whole, but can be knapped to produce a plane surface or even a fully shaped cube or sub-square cuboid. Some of the ways in which flints can be used in rubble walling are illustrated here, and there is further discussion of the different appearances that can be achieved can be found in the *Selected Churches* entry for Bishopstone (ESx).

The most common material used for facings in flint-built churches is sandstone. This comes largely from the various beds of the Lower Greensand, which outcrops north of the Downs in the central (West Sussex) section of the Park; the outcrop runs roughly east–west, but in eastern Hampshire it turns north in the Petersfield area and continues towards Farnham (Surrey). The stone goes by a variety of names, mainly taken from the locality where it was quarried. As well as dressings for flint churches it was used in

Contrasting patterns of flint masonry (from *Geology and Scenery in the SDNP*, p. 34)

its own right as a building stone, not only in churches along the line of the outcrop, but in some further south, since the stone was transported through the Downs by river, especially by the Arun and the Adur. Bands of iron-rich sandstone occur in this formation, providing building stone of noticeably darker colour.

Malmstone herringbone work in the N wall of St Paul's, Elsted

Slab of Sussex 'marble' in the porch floor of Greatham church (from *Geology and Scenery in the SDNP*, p. 9)

South and west of the Lower Greensand is a narrow outcrop of Upper Greensand, locally known as malmstone. It is typically used on the Hampshire–West Sussex border. A good example is Elsted (WSx), where a view of the outcrop can be seen beside the main road through the village.

To the north of the Lower Greensand in the central section of the Park is an area of Wealden Clay, which contains bands of limestone, a stone otherwise poorly represented in the Park. This variety is rich in fossil shells of a freshwater snail, now known by the Latin term *viviparus* (formerly *paludina*); this gives it a very lumpy appearance, but it can be smoothed and polished, giving rise to the name 'Sussex marble'. It is not normally used as a common building stone, but for decorative purposes and for objects such as the font in Trotton church (WSx) and the altar slab reused as flooring in the porch of Greatham church (WSx), and for indent slabs for memorial brasses, as at Stopham (WSx).

Resources beyond the Park

To the east of the Park, but still in Sussex, another type of sandstone occurs. The Hastings Beds cover a large area from Pevensey (ESx) in the south to Tonbridge (Kent) in the north, and from Folkestone (Kent) in the east to Horsham (WSx) in the west. This could easily be imported as a building stone into the eastern section of the Park. Another variety of sandstone is ubiquitous and well-known. Beyond the western end of the Hastings Beds area, around Horsham (WSx), the Wealden Clay contains a very fissile type of sandstone, which splits easily to form the roofing stones (stone 'slates') known as Horsham slabs. These were widely distributed throughout Sussex; though many church roofs in this material have been wholly or partially replaced in tile (e.g. the nave at Clayton, WSx), they can still be seen in the area of the Park.

The river systems of West Sussex and Hampshire form a ready access to sea-borne materials. The good limestones of the Isle of Wight have been regularly imported into the central and western sections of the Park, though stones from the heavily exploited quarries at Bembridge/Binstead and Quarr occur more frequently in churches of the coastal plain to the south. A more exotic limestone, from Caen in Normandy, was imported from the 11th century onward, and was more frequently used in West Sussex than Hampshire and more heavily on the coastal plain than in the Downs.

Horsham slab roof of St Anne's, Lewes

Church Architecture: Style, Form, Decoration

Projecting stone stripwork in the N wall of Corhampton church

There are no surviving churches in the Park from the period of St Wilfrid's mission, or indeed from the next 250 years. This may in part be the result of early churches being timber-built and subsequently replaced in stone, though there appears to have been a presumption in favour of masonry on account of its Roman connotations. To build 'in the Roman fashion (*more Romano*)', which included the use of recycled materials, such as brick and (possibly) Lavant stone, was to emphasize the links with 'official' Roman Christianity, of which St Wilfrid was an outstanding champion, as well as representing permanence, even eternity.

A possible exception is the early minster at Bishopstone (ESx). There is no clear evidence for the date of the Anglo-Saxon parts of the present church, but the survival of part of a long-and-short quoin at the north-west corner of the nave could point to a date in the late Anglo-Saxon period (roughly 950–1066). However, the south porch has been converted from an original side-chamber, or *porticus*, not inconsistent with similar chambers attached to Kentish churches of the conversion period; accessible only from inside the church, these *porticus* had varying functions, such as side chapels and burial chambers. At Bishopstone there could have been an altar against the east wall. The blocked window in the gable end and another in the north wall of the nave are small and round-headed and splayed to the interior; they are possibly, but not necessarily, early.

The **later Anglo-Saxon** period is well represented elsewhere. Key features include long-and-short quoins, pilaster strips and stripwork around openings, standing slightly proud of the wall surface, and double-splayed windows, in which the narrow aperture is not on the outside face of the wall but mid-way through the wall thickness, with a splay opening up to the exterior as well as to the interior. The quoins and stripwork can be seen at Corhampton (H), Sompting (WSx) and Woolbeding (WSx). A long-and-short quoin has been recognised at Sullington (WSx) at the north-west corner of the tower, which may be the remnant of an earlier church, though this church is not regarded as Anglo-Saxon in the standard literature. Double-splayed windows occur low down in the west tower at Singleton (WSx) (which also has a typically Anglo-Saxon gable-headed doorway to the nave at high level) and at Stoughton (WSx), one in each of the flanking *porticus*, but in both cases they are made of dressed stone rather than the plastered rubble typical of such windows elsewhere in England, and this is regarded as a mark of post-Conquest construction. The chancel arch at Stoughton is quite elaborate, with roll mouldings of the sort that appear at Bosham and Selham (both

A double-splayed window in the tower of Stoughton St Mary

WSx). The latter is a simple nave-and-chancel church of the sort that occurs frequently in the area, especially in West Sussex, for example at Hardham and Stopham. Without any date stones or documentary evidence it is difficult to know whether these churches belong to

the end of the Anglo-Saxon period or the beginning of the Norman, and the term **Saxo-Norman Overlap** has been coined to refer to the period from about the middle of the 11th century to around 1100 or even beyond, during which elements of both the Anglo-Saxon and post-Conquest building styles can be found in various combinations. (As a style, the latter is better referred to by its international name '**Romanesque**', rather than the traditional 'Norman'.)

This is not just a convenient let-out for indecisive architectural historians: there was a genuine period of transition. Even before the Norman Conquest the Romanesque style was in use in this country, if only in the new building of Westminster Abbey under Edward the Confessor, dedicated just before his death in 1065. Equally, features of apparently pre-Conquest design appear in unambiguously Romanesque buildings, for example double-splayed windows in surviving refectory walling of Lewes Priory, founded in 1078, along with herringbone masonry, a typical 'overlap' feature.

The Romanesque style proper was in full swing shortly after the Conquest, at least

Post-Conquest double-splayed windows at Lewes Priory

tall than their predecessors. Churches of greater importance (though less than that of Winchester or Chichester cathedrals) have more developed plans: at East Meon and Petersfield (H) that means a cruciform arrangement, i.e. the plan forms a Latin cross with (originally) a short chancel and transepts representing the arms, a longer nave the stem, and a tower at the point of intersection (the crossing). Initially there were no side aisles, though in both cases these were added later. These churches were also expensively provided with carved stone features, notably capitals supporting the crossing arches and intricate decoration of the arches themselves, and the equivalent parts of doors and windows.

This type of church occurs all over the country, especially where Romanesque churches replaced earlier minsters, which had been churches of some importance. At Old Shoreham (WSx) part of the Anglo-Saxon church was retained at the west end, while a central tower, transepts and a chancel were added at the east end. Another version of the cruciform plan has been recognized in the Midlands, in which there is no crossing, but simply transepts attached to the side walls of the nave,

as far as major buildings were concerned, reflecting the abrupt change in political control following the momentous Battle of Hastings. The great cathedral that was to replace the Anglo-Saxon Old Minster in Winchester was begun in 1079; the crypt, transepts and central tower show characteristic features of the first generation of Romanesque buildings.

These include door- and window-openings with semi-circular arches, but with broader, lower proportions than their pre-Conquest equivalents; with few exceptions windows are single-splayed; buttresses are obviously structural, broader than pilaster strips and coursed with the surrounding walling; and when it comes to minor buildings walls are thicker and less

Petersfield, St Peter: responds of
N arcade and chancel arch with
decorative stone carving

W door of East Meon church with
richly carved stonework

rather like Anglo-Saxon *porticus*; the Saxo-Norman Stoughton (WSx) is an example in the Park area. Further east, however, there are no comparable instances, though they might have been expected at Lewes, Beddingham or Bishopstone in East Sussex.

Pride of place, though, goes to Steyning (WSx), successor of a saint's minster and a king's burial place. Before it was reduced and remodelled around 1600 it was a grand church, planned from the beginning not only with a crossing tower and complex east end, but with integral side aisles. Plenty of high-quality carving here, too, including corbels, mouldings round arches, head stops, and pieces recalling the Anglo-Saxon past, such as some motifs on the capitals of the arch between the south aisle and the former transept, and a Saxo-Norman grave cover and another perhaps earlier.

These are a reminder of the pre-Conquest tradition of stone carving, richly represented at Sompting and intriguingly at Selham (both WSx).

Churches of lesser status, if they had towers at all, usually placed them at the west end of the nave. This custom began in the late Anglo-Saxon period (Singleton and Sompting, WSx, Jevington, ESx), and continued in the Norman period at such sites as Warnford (H) and Bishopstone

Interior of Steyning parish church looking E, showing carved arcade and chancel arches and window surrounds

Capitals supporting arch between S aisle and former transept at Steyning; the richly carved decoration of early 12th-century date is influenced by Viking styles of an earlier period

Decorative carving on arches in crossing and N transept at Old Shoreham church

with towers, where there is frequently a high-level doorway with its sill at the level of the nave wall top; there are examples at Meonstoke, Newton Valence and Easton (H) and Singleton (WSx). During the 12th century, however, vaulted stone ceilings developed, and Easton (H) is the sole example in the Park of their use: the remarkable chancel, more like a fortress than part of a church, has a square bay and an apse, both rib-vaulted. The date is around 1200 – the end of the Norman period – when simple churches were acquiring side aisles and thus connecting (ESx). An obvious local exception is the tower at East Dean (ESx), formerly a 'tower nave' to which a larger church was added on its south side, and there are five other examples in the Park of towers which are not on the east–west axis of the church.

The great Romanesque churches of SDNP almost certainly had flat wooden ceilings, of the sort that still survives in Peterborough and Ely cathedrals. Evidence for the use of roof spaces, which implies an attic floor, can be seen in churches

Sompting, St Mary: carved capitals of tower arch

Selham, St James: carved capital of chancel arch

Bishopstone, St Andrew, general view from SW

arcades inside. Selborne has arcades that show the transition from the Romanesque to the succeeding **Early English** phase of the **Gothic** style: circular piers, scalloped capitals and square abaci support the innovative plain pointed arches. The inserted N arcade at Elsted (WSx), by contrast, is still fully Romanesque, while that at Botolphs is wholly Gothic, with double-chamfered pointed arches on

moulded circular capitals, mid-13th century.

The pointed arch in a variety of forms continued in use until the end of the Gothic style in the early to mid-16th century. Romanesque forms of decoration gave way to leaf patterns and plant scrolls. Much of the development of Gothic took place in major buildings where there was a need

for rebuilds and extensions, and most local churches saw only a pale reflection of this. It is most easily recognized in the design of windows. In Anglo-Saxon and Romanesque churches windows were usually single, small and splayed, though at belfry level in towers double bell openings were used. The Gothic took the double window further, and large windows of three or more lights, subdivided by mullions,

The chancel east window at Selborne (H) has three separate lancets, and the east window of the south aisle shows the next stage in the development: three lancet-shaped lights under a super-arch. There is a similar window at nearby Newton Valence.

Then inventive tracery patterns begin to fill the area beneath the enclosing arch, developing from the mid-13th century to the mid-14th. But there are few examples of such windows in the Park, and it is as though church building came to a halt for some reason. The best example of the kind

became the norm. East windows were perhaps the most likely to be replaced, but a surprising number of churches seem to have got stuck with groups of two or three lancet windows. The progression can be seen well in the Park. Starting with the rare single-light (blocked) window at Greatham (WSx), the next stage is illustrated in the same wall, where two separate lancets were inserted either side of the early window; the interior splays almost merge to form a single embrasure.

Interior of Greatham church, looking E, showing two widely splayed windows in the end wall

Variations on the Gothic window at the E end of Selborne, St Mary

Early tracery
window in
Petworth
House chapel

Cusped intersecting tracery in the E wall of
Westdean church

Late-medieval tracery in the Perpendicular style at Rodmell, St Peter, flanked by masonry from earlier windows

Reticulated tracery in the E window of Soberton church

of tracery with a circle or circles above the arches of the lights (the **Geometrical** version of Early English) is the chapel in Petworth House (WSx), and there is a similar head to the central niche in the south transept at Soberton (H); elsewhere there are a few instances of intersecting tracery. The contribution of the **Decorated** style in the 14th century is the invention of the ogee or reverse curve, giving rise to reticulated tracery – a network of stone bars (*reticula* is Latin for a net) – an example of which can be seen in the chancel east window at Soberton (H).

From the middle of the 14th century church building and improvement seems to get going again. At Arundel (WSx) the foundation of a college of priests in 1380 led to a new church, the most sophisticated in the area; a cruciform church was built at Poynings (WSx) under the terms of the will of a man who died in 1369; and at Alfriston (ESx) there was a

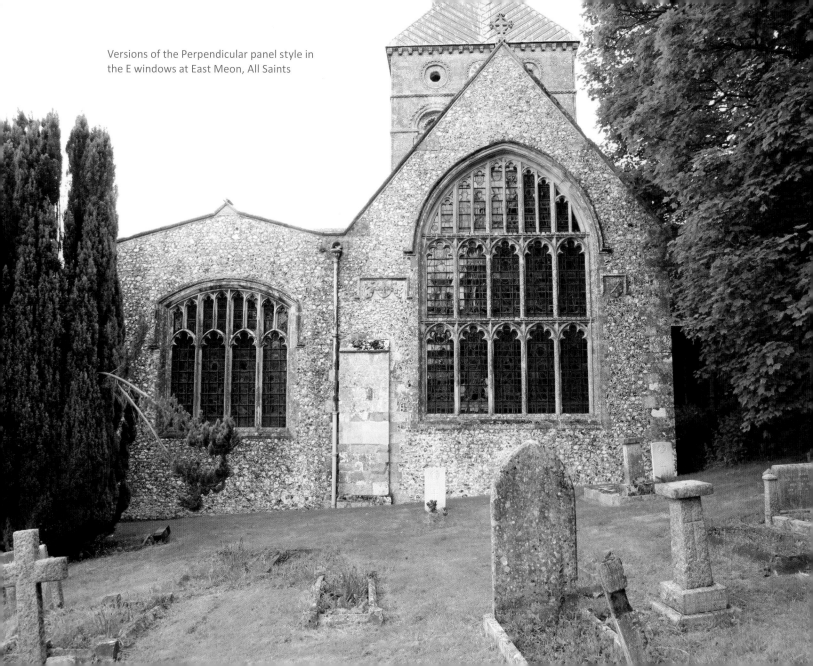

Versions of the Perpendicular panel style in the E windows at East Meon, All Saints

similar, but undated, new church. These buildings adopted the incoming sub-style of Gothic, known as **Perpendicular** on account of the rectilinear pattern of its window tracery, which became elaborate in a rather rigid way. Large panelled windows became popular everywhere, and were often used to replace existing chancel east windows. By the early 16th century severely reduced versions were available and frequently used, no doubt because they were relatively cheap. This development of Gothic window styles is difficult to illustrate from examples in our area, and Victorian rebuilding is often the culprit. At Petersfield, for example, many of the medieval windows were replaced in the 19th-century restoration, including paired lancets in the chancel south wall and multiple-light windows in the E walls of the S transept and chancel; these are illustrated in a pre-restoration watercolour (see p. 92).

'Reduced' tracery in the E window of Stopham church

Following the reform of the Anglican liturgy *c.*1550 it was a case of reduction rather than construction, and the simplified worship needs affected the interior arrangements rather than the fabric of the churches: these developments are discussed below under Furnishings and Fittings. The rise of Nonconformist places of worship took place in the context of domestic architecture, in which timber and brick were the basic materials, until the adoption of revived Gothic styles of building in the 19th century. In some instances more substantial chapels were built in a neo-Classical style, but like their Anglican equivalents – apart from the exceptional Avington (H) and Glynde (ESx) – were mainly an urban phenomenon. In neither case is it possible to write any kind of synthesis based on the few examples in the Park.

Furnishings and Fittings

The Altar and its furniture

The medieval altar was a substantial masonry structure, supporting a large rectangular slab of stone, and often attached to the east wall of the chancel – or another part of the church in the case of the subsidiary altars dedicated to saints whose intercession and support the people relied upon. These were replaced by wooden communion tables in the mid-16th century (only one per church). The work required for their demolition may be judged by the effort it took to replace them later. In 1553, early in the reign of Queen Mary, it took two men in Melton Mowbray (Leicestershire) a day and a half and several loads of stone to replace the high altar that had been removed under Edward VI in 1549 (it was taken out again in 1559 under Elizabeth I). Similar evidence can be found in the churchwardens' accounts for the combined parish of St Andrew and St Michael in Lewes (ESx), though there is not the same direct reference to the substantial nature of the traditional altar. Big altar slabs were less easily disposed of than the often rubble masonry of the supporting structure. Sometimes they were broken up, but often reused as doorsteps or even hidden under the church floor. Because of the history of continued Catholicism at Arundel (WSx), there are still three medieval slabs in the Fitzalan and Lady Chapels, but otherwise the survival rate in SDNP is very small; one possible example is the Sussex marble slab in the porch floor at Greatham (WSx), though this may equally be a brass indent turned upside down, and there is another at West Chiltington.

A lot of furniture associated with the altar has survived, however, by dint of being built into the fabric of the building. At Newton Valence (H) there is a triple-arched 15th-century reredos built into the sill of the chancel east window, which no doubt originally held three statues, and the window is flanked by tall niches. In the chancel at Ditchling (ESx) the east window itself formed the reredos; it is flanked by two tall blind arches. Meonstoke (H) is similar and has also a minor panelled reredos at window sill level. Most impressive is the evidence in the south

Altar reredos in the embrasure of the E chancel window of Meonstoke, St Andrew, and flanking image niches

transept at Soberton (H), where there is not only an architectural niche between the two east windows but considerable traces of a scheme of mural paintings.

Reredoses often took the form of a dropped window sill, providing an area of plain masonry which could be painted with an appropriate background. There are examples of this in the transepts at North Stoke (WSx), a church which gives a good impression of the liturgical arrangements of a late medieval church

Soberton, Sts Peter & Paul, E wall of S transept with altar reredos recess; note the substantial remains of medieval wall painting

Soberton, Sts Peter & Paul, E wall of S transept, remains of painting on window splay

as a whole. In the chancel the east window is flanked by image brackets mounted on decorative corbels, which is comparable with the Ditchling recesses. In the south wall is a group of sedilia and piscina; the sedilia were the seats for the clergy serving the Mass, and the piscina the basin with drain which received the water used for washing the priest's hands before and after handling the elements of Holy Communion. There is a remarkable depiction of this procedure in the former chapel of one of the houses, known as Rode Poort, which surround the courtyard of Utrecht Cathedral (Netherlands).

Piscinas are one of the commonest surviving forms of evidence for the position of the medieval altar; there are examples at Sompting and the Mardens (WSx), Alfriston (ESx), and Easton and Newton Valence (H). The 13th-century recess at Newton Valence incorporates the head and part of the shaft of an earlier piscina, known as

North Stoke, St Mary, showing drop sill and piscina

North Stoke, St Mary, view into chancel with piscina and sedilia, and into S transept with drop window sill for reredos; between them reredos recess for minor nave altar

Alfriston, St Andrew, piscina and sedilia in chancel

Utrecht, Netherlands, piscina with detail of painted back panel (see p. 49)

Newton Valence, St Mary, miniature pillar piscina incorporated in later wall-niche piscina

Chilcomb, St Andrew, pillar piscina

a pillar piscina, a well attested form from the late 11th and 12th centuries, designed to be free-standing and positioned over a floor drain near the altar. The pillar piscina at Chilcomb (H) is complete and still stands free; its head has waterleaf capitals, indicating a date in the late 12th century. The most intriguing piscina, however, is at Petworth: it is located in the first-floor room over the north transept, the private 'pew' of the owners of Petworth House. It presumably functioned in relation to an altar at this level during the Middle Ages. What the drainage arrangements were is not known.

Returning to sedilia, these are not so common as piscinas, which probably means that they were less often incorporated into the fabric; wooden seats were probably the norm. Further built-in examples occur, however, at Alfriston and Ditchling (ESx) and Poynings (WSx).

Easter Sepulchres

The Easter Sepulchre was typically a confection of timber, metalwork and cloth hangings, which represented Christ's tomb and was used from Good Friday to Easter Day to keep the consecrated Host, representing Christ's Body, in a re-enactment of the events of Easter. The sepulchre was placed close to the altar on the north side of the chancel. In some cases there was a structural recess in the north wall of the chancel in which the sepulchre itself could be erected; the cost of installing such recesses was often borne by individuals, who would have their own tomb chest incorporated into it, specifying in their wills that this should act as a base for the sepulchre. The sepulchres themselves could be easily destroyed when the ritual ceased to be practised in the mid-16th century, but the niches often survived simply as tomb recesses, or by dint of being blocked up and plastered over. Actual physical destruction of the architectural features also took place, as the example of Berwick (ESx) shows: the stonework, including a large canopy in the Decorated style, was reconstructed in the 1850s from fragments unearthed in the churchyard.

Elsewhere in East Sussex there is an example at Alfriston, with an ogee arch and pinnacles matching those of the sedilia opposite, and a similar one at Westdean, but the supposed sepulchre recess at Bishopstone is thought to be too early (12th-century, with roll moulding) and thus just a large aumbry (wall cupboard). West Sussex has three examples: at Singleton there is a tomb with a flat canopy against the north chancel wall; another canopied tomb in the same position at Sompting; and West Chiltington has a plain recess with a segmental arch. In the Hampshire

Westdean, All Saints, Easter Sepulchre in N wall of chancel

Alfriston, St Andrew, tomb recess in N chancel wall with later figures

part of SDNP the only possible sepulchre recess is at Meonstoke, where there are tomb recesses with segmental arches on either side of the chancel; that on the north side may have been intended to house a sepulchre. Apart from that, there is a documentary reference in 1552 to the destruction of a sepulchre at Hambledon.

Screens & rood lofts

From at least the 13th century the chancel was separated from the public part of the church by a screen. In those parts of the country where these survive they are generally of wood, though there are a few stone screens. At the top of the screen a gallery, known as a rood loft, developed in the later medieval period; its main purpose was to give access to the rood – the great suspended crucifix – which hung in front of the chancel arch. The arch itself, or part of it, was filled with a timber partition, on which was painted a background to the rood, often a Doom or Last Judgement. Most of these elements were destroyed in the course of the 16th century and later, though the screens themselves survived in a fair number of cases. But this is not so in the area of the Park, where there are few survivals of screen-work of any sort, and the best evidence for the medieval arrangement is the surviving rood loft stair at Singleton (WSx). Internally there are open doorways at both levels, and externally there is a thickening of the wall in the angle between the north aisle and the chancel to accommodate the stairs.

Easton, St Mary, interior access to rood loft stair

Singleton, St John the Evangelist, interior access to rood loft stair

There is similar evidence at Easton (H) and, though less obviously, at Soberton (H). There is a screen across the chancel arch at Berwick (ESx), which appears to be 13th-century, but it is covered with Bloomsbury Group paint, and it is difficult to be sure that it is not a 19th-century copy. Late 13th-century, too, the remains of the screen at Old Shoreham (WSx), which has narrow lights and trefoil heads. Parts of the church other than the chancel were commonly screened off to form separate

Singleton, St John the Baptist, wall thickening between chancel and nave to accommodate rood loft stair

chapels in the Middle Ages; there are remains of 14th-century work at Poynings (WSx) and Rodmell (ESx). At Ditchling (ESx) there are screens of around 1946 by the local architect J L Denman. There is no screen-work in the Hampshire section of SDNP.

Fonts

The *Life of St Wilfrid* recounts that after the saint's successful preaching 'many thousands . . . were baptised in one day'. It does not say where or how. The earlier baptism of King Æthelwalh had taken place in the Midlands, where he was received by the Mercian king *de fonte*. This is usually translated as 'from the font', but it is highly unlikely that fonts as we know them had been introduced at this early date. The basic meaning of the Latin word is spring, well, fountain, and could refer to any naturally occurring water source. No doubt the king and his people were baptized in rivers, or even in the sea; this would be a convenient medium for the mass baptism of adults, and in keeping with tradition established elsewhere in Anglo-Saxon England. It could also be seen as an allusion to Christ's baptism in the River Jordan.

On the continent, particularly in southern France and Italy, free-standing purpose-built baptisteries had developed, with a masonry tank embedded in the floor, entered by steps and provided with bench seating. These were appropriate for adult baptism, and usually attached to a cathedral, since the rite was administered by the bishop. The best-known example is at St John Lateran, the cathedral of Rome. There is slight evidence for their use in Roman Britain, and the only baptistery known from Anglo-Saxon England has left no tangible remains above ground. Fonts developed in response to the adoption of infant baptism – they are hardly practical for adult baptism – which happened in pre-Conquest England. There are very few, however, that can be claimed stylistically to be of Anglo-Saxon date, and there are not enough of them to average out at even one per county. There may be several reasons for the lack of survivals. One is that some fonts were probably made of perishable materials, rather than stone: manuscript illustrations show that they could be wooden and stave-built, rather like cut-down barrels. Another is that because there were as yet no parish

Lewes, St Anne, font

Poynings, Holy Trinity, font

At all events, there was a sudden upsurge in font-making in the late 11th and 12th centuries, which coincides exactly with the consolidation of the parochial system. There are many more fonts carved in the Romanesque style than all others together; once a parish had one, it would be replaced only in the case of irreparable damage or a desire to match the style of the church itself if there were a Gothic rebuild (as, for example, at Arundel, WSx).

The general run of Romanesque fonts is well represented at St Anne's, Lewes (ESx), and Corhampton (H), while of the same period there are Purbeck 'table-type' fonts with shallow arched decoration at Meonstoke (H) and Rodmell (ESx). There is a tapering tub at Woolbeding (WSx). East Meon has one of the few highly ornate examples in black marble from Tournai (Belgium). In addition to Arundel, as noted above, there are 14th-century fonts at Alfriston and Jevington (ESx) and Poynings (WSx), and fonts in the Perpendicular style at Petersfield (H) and Willingdon (ESx). At Parham (WSx) is a very rare example of a 14th-century lead font with an inscription repeating '✠IHS Nazar'.

churches, authority to baptize delegated by the bishop would have resided in the minsters, of which there were far fewer; so fewer fonts (or baptismal tanks, if they were still being used) would have been required.

During the Commonwealth period, Puritan sentiment led to the removal and often the destruction of medieval fonts, especially those with Christian imagery, a plain domestic-style basin being held sufficient for the purpose. Some were reinstated later or (in the 19th century) replaced by

Avington, St Mary, font

East Meon, All Saints, Tournai marble font

new ones in the Gothic style. In the 17th and 18th centuries fonts in a Classical baluster style were favoured, particularly in new church buildings, such as Avington (H) and Glynde (ESx)

Parham, St Peter, lead font

Avington, St Mary, interior looking E

Post-Reformation furnishings

These two post-medieval churches are still complete with their furniture, and offer a guide to the norms of the period: Avington (H) and Glynde (ESx), both dating from the 1760s. Avington has a full-width reredos with panels displaying the then obligatory Ten Commandments, Lord's Prayer and Creed; a metal communion rail; enclosed pews and a three-decker pulpit with an elaborate tester (sounding board); a west gallery; and timber panelling throughout, complete with hat pegs. At Glynde the reredos is restricted to the width of the east window embrasure, leaving room for pews on either side facing the altar table, and has no commandments board; the communion rail is similarly restricted, is wooden and has narrow turned spindles; the west gallery is later, 1841, but stylistically in keeping.

These arrangements were appropriate for a form of worship in which priority was given not to Holy Communion but to the Word of God as read from scripture (from the middle level of the pulpit) and preached, often at great length (from the top level). In the same period (17th–early 19th centuries) the interiors of many medieval churches were adapted to the

Bishop's Waltham, St Peter, post-Reformation pulpit

same end. West galleries were used by the local band to provide music for the services (Avington had a barrel organ, which no doubt deprived the musicians of their fees), as in Thomas Hardy's *Under the Greenwood Tree*, but these galleries went out of fashion shortly after the

one at Glynde was installed. Examples can be found at Lewes St Anne (ESx) and Idsworth (H: 1912!). Idsworth also has furnishings of the type under discussion; so have Droxford and Soberton (H), and Greatham, Poynings, Parham and Woolbeding (WSx); Parham has a fireplace in the north transeptal annex. East Dean (ESx) and Bishop's Waltham and East Meon (H) have pulpits of 1623, 1626 and 1706 respectively.

Glass

Most of the churches in the *Selected* list have 'stained' (i.e. coloured) glass in their windows, much of it of 19th- and 20th-century date, because of the destruction of much medieval glass at or after the Reformation. Space does not allow a listing of all that is worth seeing; only medieval survivals and unusual glazing schemes can be mentioned here. North Stoke (WSx) has a small panel showing the Coronation of the Virgin, probably early 14th-century; Poynings (WSx) has true stained glass figures of an Annunciation, early 15th; Rodmell (ESx) has a small 15th-century crucifixus, originally part of a Trinity scene, also stained glass; Woolbeding (WSx) two windows with 16th-century continental

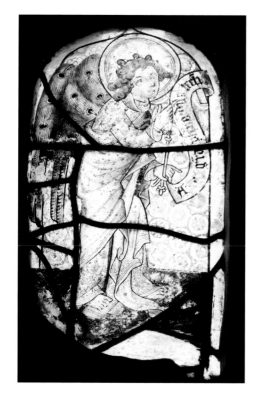

Poynings, Holy Trinity, N transept E window, two lights showing Annunciation, stained glass, early 15th-century

East Meon, All Saints, glass in chancel E window

glass; Alfriston (ESx) has various medieval fragments and a rare St Christopher of 1902 by Max Balfour; Glynde (ESx) reset Netherlandish panels of the 16th and 17th centuries; Firle (ESx) has some 15th-century glass and a Piper window in the Gage Chapel, 1985; and Willingdon (ESx) has a wide variety of glazing, including heraldic glass of 1622 (reset) pertaining to the Parker family, whose monuments are a feature of the church interior. At East Meon (H) the glass of the east window is by Ninian Comper.

Willingdon, St Mary, heraldic glass

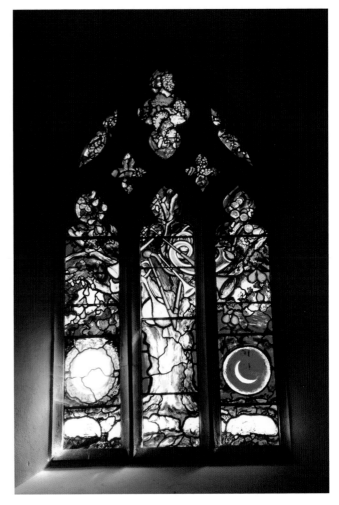

West Firle, St Peter, John Piper glass in Gage chapel E window

Wall Painting
(RM-G)

Places mentioned in the text of this section are in West Sussex unless otherwise stated.

The construction of a medieval church was completed only when the interior walls (in Downland churches, normally of rough rubble) were plastered, twelve consecration crosses were painted at important locations within – outside, they could be incised – and a painterly scheme applied to the plaster overall. At its simplest this could be quite perfunctory: often a stylized masonry-pattern, with or without repeated decorative motifs, maybe stencilled. But even in humble churches there seems to have been a strong urge to include figurative subjects based on Biblical or other sacred themes – thus continuing of course a tradition that goes back to the earliest days of Christianity, as witnessed by the painted walls of a room evidently used as a chapel (4th-century) in the Roman villa at Lullingstone, Kent. These could form elaborate narrative cycles – specially in the case of saints' Lives

Clayton, St John the Baptist, interior looking E with chancel arch and Christ in Majesty

– and this is tantalizing to the present-day visitor trying to make sense of the fragments that are so often all that survive; in the words of Clive Rouse (the greatest British restoration expert during much of the 20th century), we should 'treat them like the small, individual pieces of a great jigsaw-puzzle'; 'every piece may provide important evidence and information

when we have lost so much'. These losses derive from three main causes: natural processes of decay, particularly when damp affects the adherence of plaster to the wall-surface, or when paintwork fades; the iconoclasm of the Reformation, when paintings were routinely whitewashed, sometimes attacked; restoration and rebuilding of churches, mostly in the 19th century, when old plaster was all too often knocked off the walls.

In the South Downs area, however, we are uniquely fortunate in having several schemes of wall painting unmatched in their completeness and early date. They are: Clayton; Hardham; Coombes; West Chiltington – to these one might have added Plumpton (ESx), Keymer and Westmeston (ESx) were it not for the destruction wrought by Victorian restorers (at Plumpton, however, significant amounts of original painting have since been discovered). Plumpton relates quite closely to Clayton – it may have possessed a cruder, more 'provincial' version of the former's scheme – while Westmeston (judging by a drawing) had iconography in common with Hardham.

West Chiltington – not as early as the others: its first extant painting must date from the later 12th century – represents a remarkable 'gallery' of schemes from all subsequent medieval periods.

Why is 'earliness' of special significance? For two main reasons. One is historical: though there is documentary evidence for Anglo-Saxon wall painting (and on the

Plumpton, St Michael, Heavenly City (drawing by E Clive Rouse, 1955)

Continent such painting exists in unbroken, if rather tenuous, tradition at least from Carolingian times), there is virtually no survival of unambiguously pre-Conquest wall painting in England. Only two flying angels in the church of Nether Wallop near Winchester (H), and a painted stone excavated in the city itself, seem to have been generally accepted as such. Of

course there is plenty of surviving Saxon manuscript illumination, not to mention stone carving, so this is a particularly tantalizing lacuna in a record that might help us understand the rather bumpy transition in English art from the Saxon to the fully-fledged Romanesque around the time of the Norman Conquest. The other reason is technical. Early wall painting in England (as elsewhere) utilizes the technique of true fresco. This necessitates application of the pigment, suspended in lime water, day by day on fresh plaster before it dries out. A chemical bond between the plaster and the pigment takes place, securing the image in a way that secco painting, on dry plaster, cannot match. In various places, notably Coombes (see front cover), fresco and (later) secco images can be seen side-by-side: the latter have deteriorated much more than the former. So early, fresco paintwork retains its vividness and no doubt closeness to what the original painter wished.

Fresco disappeared in England (as in all Western, but not Orthodox, Europe till the Renaissance) by the end of the 12th century. It should be noted that there are intermediate possibilities between fresco and secco techniques (e.g. finishing off with secco painting on a frescoed base), and laboratory testing is needed to establish the technique beyond doubt. True fresco, with its obligation on the painter to work fast before the plaster dried out, encouraged a bold, free, unfussy handling of the medium, contributing to the exceptional quality of the three major schemes mentioned above. In Clayton and Coombes we can see, close up, the very brush-strokes made nearly 1000 years ago. Later artists however, working on dry (or superficially damped) plaster, could not only take their time in producing more intricate effects, but had a wider range of pigments at their disposal (they could use metallic pigments unsuitable for fresco). The early fresco-painter's palette was confined, with rare additions, to red and yellow oxides occurring naturally in the Lower Greensand beds north of the Downs, together with lime white and charcoal black. These reds and yellows, however, are wonderfully varied, from purple to pink, from brownish to cream, even occasionally greenish. Particularly at Clayton and Coombes they are mixed or juxtaposed with white to virtuoso effect (often in striped garments). Moreover a quite convincing blue could be obtained through an effect of light called 'Rayleigh

Idsworth, St Hubert, chancel, Herod's Feast

scattering' by mixing a small quantity of charcoal particles into white – a useful recourse at a time when the only available 'true blue', lapis lazuli or 'ultramarine', was rare and expensive. A copper-based bluish green appears in a few haloes at Hardham.

Medieval wall painting was not exactly an anonymous art – quite a few painters' names (and the fees they earned) are known from accounts kept by cathedrals and palaces, particularly in the later Middle Ages. But the comparatively grand schemes involved represent a different sphere from that of the Downland parish

churches. In the absence of records, we have to guess from the physical evidence how patronage operated, how the content of painting-schemes came to be chosen, who the artists were and how they worked. Small teams of painters – more likely laymen than monks – would have to be hired to adorn the church as soon as it was built, enlarged or renovated. They would no doubt have had pattern-books, but it is clear they did not copy them slavishly. When parish funds ran out, a scheme could be temporally halted and resumed later (this seems to have happened with the two nave walls at West Chiltington).

Biblical subjects and saints tended to cede ground as the medieval period progressed to moralistic, often fanciful depictions of allegorical subjects (e.g. The Seven Deadly Sins and Seven Works of Mercy, late 14th-century, at Arundel; the same again, rather later and in more complex format, with elements of the Last Judgement, at Trotton). There are astonishing early 14th-century episodes from the life of St John the Baptist, including Herod's Feast, with possible hunting scenes above, on the chancel wall at Idsworth (H).

Subjects of contemporary relevance, often heraldic, start to appear: Trotton also features donor portraits and heraldry of the locally important Camoys family (early 15th century); Boxgrove, shields of the de la Warrs. But such relevance may of course remain obscure to us. What can we make, for example, of the 'Solomonic [endless] knot', surrounded by fleur-de-lys symbols, high up on an inconspicuous wall at West Chiltington? Is the image somehow to do with Edward III's claim on the throne of France and founding of the Order of the Garter in the mid-14th century? Why did someone go to the trouble to put it there? There is another rather distorted fleur-de-lys, the only visible 14th-century painted fragment in Buncton – again, with what significance?

More generally, we can be sure that the choice of scenes from the large repertory of Christian thematics was never unmotivated, and must have involved serious discussion between patrons and painters. Sometimes we can see from the church's dedication how the choice came about; more often it is now irretrievable. Was it more likely that a rural church would reflect its congregation's working lives in the subjects depicted: the Labours of the Months, for example, on the Hardham chancel-arch; the unusual emphasis on the role of the shepherds in the Nativity cycle at West Chiltington? And once the subjects of painting have been decided, what logic lies behind their disposition within the church's space? Hardham – with around 40 surviving scenes, an unparalleled number, would be a good place to begin such an investigation: is it significant that, from the chancel, one's eye is first taken by a remarkable cycle showing Adam and Eve, while on the far wall, through the arch, scenes of Hell could be glimpsed? All such questions had answers that once may have been obvious, but are no longer so.

One intriguing problem concerns the teams of painters who fulfilled the commissions: did they form enduring workshops with distinctive approaches still to be appreciated in what has survived to our days? This has been much discussed in relation to the early paintings at Clayton, Hardham, Coombes and Plumpton (together with some now-lost schemes)

West Chiltington, St Mary, endless knot with fleurs-de-lys, © Lisa Fisher

Coombes church, soffit of chancel arch, Atlas figure, © Roger Wilmshurst

mentioned earlier. Over 100 years ago the notable Sussex antiquarian and restorer P M Johnston observed that not only did the newly-uncovered paintings at Hardham and Clayton have features in common, but that both had belonged to the Cluniac Priory of Lewes (ESx) at times in the 12th century. Thus arose the term 'Lewes Group' or 'Lewes School' that has haunted debate ever since, giving rise to such fanciful scenarios as a team of Burgundian painters travelling from church to church owned by the Priory (very many, at one time or another). However, the discovery (1950s) of paintings at Coombes – not a Priory possession – that were in all respects closer to Clayton than those at Hardham undermined the Lewes connection, which was already looking shaky for several other reasons. The terms are often still encountered, but seldom in serious scholarship. Do the monuments we have mentioned even constitute a 'group'? Given there could have been at least 100 parish churches in the Downland region, all decorated, by the end of the 11th century, any answer is conjectural. If we do regard the ones that survive or were recorded as belonging to a special category, the construction of the buildings themselves can give us guidance as to how they are related. Clayton has all the characteristics of a quite ambitious Anglo-Saxon church; if it, and its coeval paintings, are to be regarded as post-Conquest, they can only be improbably archaic. Coombes and Plumpton give little away; there are few obvious datable features, though the stonework of Plumpton seems hastily thrown together in a manner indicating the surge in church construction soon after the Conquest. The surviving north wall paintings copy Clayton, but crudely: Clayton's refinement has degenerated into a set of mannerisms. If indeed there was a long-lasting workshop, whose earliest known product was Clayton, and not merely a set of stylistic techniques and commonplaces of unknown (but not, it seems, Norman) provenance, then Plumpton appears to represent a third generation of painters. In between, we may suppose, comes Coombes. It has sometimes been classed as a Saxon building, though the evidence is slight: long-and-short quoins are built into the west wall, but this had to be stabilized after the tower fell down. The fragmented, but wonderfully vivid frescoes follow the 'striped style' – a painterly resource characteristic of the mid-11th century, but going back to antiquity – of Clayton, yet the figure style shows differences: bodies are bent into S or Z shapes, modelled with hatching (quite uncharacteristic of high Romanesque), while we encounter a wonderful repertory of gesticulating hands – and, in the case of the memorable Coombes 'Atlas' figure, a grimacing mouth.

In concentrating on the superb paintings exemplified by Clayton, we should not forget that other early schemes once existed. Excavations of early churches at

Plate 22.

COCKING CH: SUSSEX: Painting on Splay of Norman Window.

P. M. JOHNSTON. DEL.

Cocking church, splay of 12th-century window; Nativity scene (drawing by P M Johnston, c.1900)

Both schemes make virtuoso use of bold decorative borders inherited from antiquity: Greek key patterns, a great mid-wall foliage scroll at Clayton (whose motif crops up at Plumpton and Coombes, oddly located in window splays).

Hardham is very different: as a building, somehow not quite Saxon, not fully Norman; its paintings – in several cycles, distinctly different in character – likewise. The angels above the chancel arch are poised in what has been called the Anglo-Saxon 'anguished stoop'; elsewhere we witness windblown garments worthy of the 'Winchester style' of c.1000, and the unparalleled expressionism of the naked Adam and Eve. But most of the figure painting is perfunctory, with no attempt at modelling or expressive gesture: run-of-the-mill Romanesque, in fact. Different hands, apparently representing different backgrounds, were at work. The traditional pairing with Clayton is a historical accident; out of some 40 scenes Clayton and Hardham share not one. The only common feature is the strange 'architectural' motif of small, apparently stilted arches, also found at Coombes, 'sealing off' one scene from another at Hardham. No-one has ever attempted to explain it (it produces a curiously antique, Mediterranean and urban effect); it may well have been a local peculiarity.

Angmering and the lost village of Bargham nearby have yielded fragments of painted plaster; so has Lewes Priory (the largest such fragment, *c*.2 inches square, shows no resemblance to Clayton/Coombes). A fairly large painted area, hard to decipher but showing a chevron design, was recently discovered on Saxon-period masonry in Bishopstone (ESx). At Ford, near Arundel, a fine consecration cross in a roundel was found by Johnston on very early masonry; unaware of fresco in Sussex, he was puzzled by the thick, 'mastic'-like impasto. At Binsted, facing splays of a Norman window show a female saint and a strange, three-headed Tree of Life; while a similar splay at Cocking retains a delightful image of shepherd, star, angel and barking dog.

From the 13th century onwards there are many more survivals (one may single out West Chiltington, Amberley, Catherington, Southease (ESx), Trotton; two East Sussex parish churches north of Brighton, Patcham and Preston, had extensive remains, now much damaged).

In the early 16th century, just before the Reformation, the notable Chichester artist Lambert Bernard (who also did wall paintings in domestic settings in Amberley and Chichester) painted a singularly joyous foliage design supporting de la Warr shields at Boxgrove, as well as their astonishing chantry within the nave.

Thereafter, wall painting was confined to religious texts and royal coats-of-arms until the 19th century brought a revival of interest in its possibilities, as well as those of the closely-related genre of decorative tile-work (fine Morris examples at Findon and Clapham). But even the best Victorian wall painting was undervalued, left uncleaned and even obliterated in the 20th-century. Washington church is an instructive example: still partly 14th century, but otherwise rather successfully rebuilt in the 1860s, it acquired an astonishing all-over decoration in the 1880s, full of 'high Victorian vigour' (Nairn & Pevsner). This was covered in 'magnolia emulsion' in 1962, and except for highly accomplished roundels in the chancel, remains so, even though the emulsion is by now blistering.

In the 20th century Bishop Bell of Chichester championed mural painting. His Sussex commissions of the refugee painter Hans Feibusch are outside our area (Brighton, Eastbourne); but his best-known endeavour is at Berwick (ESx), where Vanessa Bell (no relation), her son Quentin and Duncan Grant produced a large-scale scheme, sometimes criticized for sentimentality, yet an honourable venture. Alas, though, what passes as genuine wall painting was done (at Kenneth Clark's urging) on removable plaster-board.

Medieval wall painting is an astonishing art, an indissoluble melding of the architectural and the painterly. In parish churches it was a rare example of an art both by and for the people: a form with which they would be familiar for a lifetime,

Washington, St Mary, late 19th-century painted roundel, © Kevin Newman

Berwick, St Michael and All Angels, interior facing E

expounded no doubt from the pulpit, but transcending didactic purposes to evoke the heavenly presence within the sacred building. It is hard now of course to recapture the all-embracing quality, the sense of awe that a fully realized scheme of painting must once have produced (a tip for modern visitors: locate the church's light switches, or bring a good torch).

Not only has the legacy of this art been inadequately evaluated – it has not even been fully explored. In Clayton, a place of international significance, the chancel remains covered in cement rendering, though clearance of a small patch decades ago revealed traces of the same paintwork as in the nave. At Eastergate, known early paintings were long ago covered over.

Facsimile copies of the destroyed Keymer paintings were made in the 19th century: where are they now? The whitewashed interiors of many small ancient churches could reveal treasures. But who will pay? Discovering and maintaining such paintings is hardly the dream of an impoverished parish.

Monuments and Memorials

Commemoration of the dead goes back to the earliest days of Christianity in Anglo-Saxon England, but there is no equivalent in this region of the headstones that have survived on Holy Island (or Lindisfarne, Northumberland) and other sites in the North-East, some of which are inscribed with the name of the person commemorated. The few pre-Conquest monuments that there are in the Park and surrounding area are much later – late Anglo-Saxon or Saxo-Norman – and anonymous. There are two grave covers in the porch of Steyning church (WSx); one of these has low-relief carving which appears to represent a stylised roof with hipped gables. With the coffin below (possibly also made of stone but no longer extant) it would have formed a 'little house of the dead', a description sometimes applied to tombs, mausolea and shrines.

Similar stones are known at Stedham and Chithurst, on the northern fringe of the

Steyning parish church, pre-Conquest grave cover

Park west of Midhurst (WSx), and it is likely that they came from one of the quarries in that area which are named in Domesday Book. Of the same general period is a carved slab at Jevington (ESx), which is sometimes claimed as a grave cover, but the modern specialist literature describes it merely as 'figural panel'.

Shortly after the Conquest William de Warenne founded the Priory of St Pancras just outside Lewes (ESx). He and his wife Gundrada were buried there (she died in 1085) and their remains were discovered when the railway line was constructed in 1845. They had been reburied around the middle of the 12th century when the monastery was rebuilt and grave covers provided posthumously. In the church of St John the Baptist, Southover (which is on the site of the former priory guest house), are two lead cists, which had contained the remains; these are now beneath Gundrada's gravestone in the south chapel of the church. This is an elaborately carved piece of Tournai marble, which is decorated with palmette ornament and has a long inscription extolling her virtues, and commending her to St Pancras, the priory's patron saint. Also found on the priory site and housed in Southover church

is the torso of a knight in Purbeck marble, mid-13th century; the remainder of the monument is missing. There is a more complete, though defaced, knight's effigy of similar date in the tower of Sullington church (WSx).

In the tower of Bishopstone church (ESx), is a small 12th-century slab with roundels defined by rope mouldings; in the roundels are relief carvings, one of them a pair of birds drinking from an urn, a motif inherited from the Roman period. In East Dean church (ESx), there is another 13th-century piece, later than the Southover knight, a slab which supposedly bears the arms of the Bardolph family. Late 13th century, too, the effigy of a lady at Droxford (H). There seem to be no surviving monuments of the 14th century, but the Fitzalan Chapel at Arundel (WSx) makes up for this in the 15th with a series of tomb chests to successive Earls of Arundel. The earliest is to Thomas, the 5th Earl, who died in 1415. This is a tomb chest with recumbent effigies of the earl and his wife, all made of alabaster, probably from Derbyshire. The monument to the 9th Earl (d.1487) is larger and more elaborate, and served also as a chantry chapel. It is of Sussex marble and the decoration still Gothic. This suggests one of the motives – apart from self-promotion – for the expenditure of significant sums of money on personalised memorials of this sort: the remembrance of future generations would add to the formal prayers on behalf of the soul of the deceased.

In the Fitzalan Chapel there are also brasses: at the west end, two 15th-century priests, and further east a man and wife (incomplete) and a small figure in armour. Of the same date-range and later, a series of brasses in Stopham church (WSx), several in Sussex marble indents, commemorating members of the Barttelot family. They begin in the nave with John

stone carries a kneeling figure in 17th-century costume, which is quite at variance with the style of the Latin inscription immediately below.

The 16th century is represented by brasses to the Shelley family in Clapham church (WSx) – John (d.1526) with his wife, and

(d.1428), another John (d.1453), Richard (d.1462) and William (d.1601, aged 97) and end in the chancel with Richard (d.1614). Despite the dates of death, the first two brasses were apparently made in London in the 1460s and 1470s. They each show man and wife with an inscription (in Latin in the 15th century, in English in the 17th) and heraldic shields giving the family's marriage alliances. The earlier brasses were 'restored' in the 17th century and additional plates were surface mounted, one in particular showing two standing male figures in contemporary dress, which contrasts interestingly with the 15th-century dress of the main figures. William's

Stopham, St Mary, a Barttelot brass in Sussex marble indent, with detail of brass plate added later

later brasses of the same century on the chancel south wall, but more importantly at (West) Firle (ESx). Here there is a mixture of monument types, from plain brasses to sculpted alabaster compositions and tomb chests bearing brasses. The simple brasses are in the floor at the end of the north aisle and in the nave; they commemorate members of the Gage family, whose dates of death run from 1476 to 1638. Then in the family chapel there are three alabaster monuments in the form of tomb chests, one to Sir John, who died in 1556, with recumbent effigies, and two others with brasses. All appear to have been made in 1595 by a Huguenot, Gerard Johnson or Garret Jansen, whose drawings survive at Firle Place and are annotated with the correspondence between him and his patron. The Firle monuments span the pre- and post-Reformation periods; the continuation of the tradition of commemoration was driven by families such as the Gages and the Howards at Arundel, who of course remained Roman Catholic. Its continuation in Protestant circles, even though prayers for the dead had been declared superstitious, suggests that there was nevertheless still a popular belief that remembrance would in some way

West Firle, St Peter, Gage family tomb, 1595

confer immortality. But apart from that the demonstration of social status and the exercise of social control were important factors in the continued erection of tombs and monuments, often at great expense.

The eastern end of the Park is rich in monuments of the late 16th/early 17th century. At Willingdon (ESx), now a suburb of Eastbourne, memorials to the Parker family can be found in the family chapel,

the chancel and the side aisles; they run from 1598 to 1727.

In the chancel of nearby Westdean (ESx) there is a large standing wall monument in alabaster to William Thomas (d.1639/40). The figures of William and his wife face each other across a prayer-desk; flanking columns support a pedimented canopy and are themselves flanked by angels.

Willingdon, St Mary, memorial in cartouche form, 1700

Westdean, All Saints, elaborate wall monument, 1639

Apart from the Fitzalan monuments at Arundel, West Sussex has nothing comparable to offer. Potentially the Cowdray monuments could fill the bill, but they are not numerous and the best of them has suffered from being moved – as they all were – from Midhurst to Easebourne (WSx). The earliest is that to David Owen, who died in 1535, an alabaster ordered 40 years before. The most imposing is that to the first Viscount

Montague (d.1592); he kneels above the recumbent effigies of his two wives, and below them are figures of their children. The figures have been rearranged and the monument has lost its corner obelisks;

Willingdon, St Mary, wall monument, 1726

the Wriothesley monument at Titchfield (H) shows what it should have looked like. Early Victorian sculpture is also represented at Easebourne: two seated figures in identical niches, one to William Poyntz (d.1840), made in 1848, and the other to his wife Elizabeth (d.1830), made in 1838 by the well-known sculptor Sir Francis Chantrey.

A few miles to the east, Petworth has a variety of monuments, the earliest to John Dawtrey (d.1542) in the north-east chapel, somewhat garishly repainted to give an impression of the original colour scheme. In the chancel an early work by John Flaxman commemorating John Wickins (d.1783), and in the north aisle the seated life-size figure of George, 3rd Earl of

Egremont, which has been compared with the figure of Wilberforce in Westminster Abbey.

One of the earliest monuments in the Hampshire section of the Park is a damaged Purbeck marble tomb in the south transept of Soberton church (H), supposedly of John Newport (d.1521). Also in the transept, to the right of the arch leading to the nave, a Baroque cartouche for Barbara Howe (d.1698) with an inscription in cursive (i.e. handwriting) script; and in the north aisle an important wall monument to Thomas Lewis (d.1747), by the well-known Flemish sculptor Peter Scheemakers, who was active in London from about 1730 until he retired in 1771.

At Warnford (H) there is early 17th-century work commemorating members of the Neale family, who owned the estate in the previous century: two alabaster monuments to William (d.1601) and Sir Thomas (d.1621), the latter with three stepped recumbent effigies, a coffered canopy, and the usual children on the tomb chest.

The monuments at Bishop's Waltham are mainly 18th-century, and include one to

Petworth, St Mary: monument in NE chapel, 1542

Soberton, Sts Peter & Paul, Baroque cartouche, 1628

Warnford, Our Lady, alabaster monument, 1621

Bishop's Waltham, St Peter, wall monument with additional tablet bearing maker's name, 1753

Avington, St Mary, Marchioness of Carnarvon's monument, 1768

Jane Wright (d.1753), a pedimented tablet with a separate stone signed by James Stubington. This is a rare instance where the name of a local craftsman is known. A few years after the death of Jane Wright, Margaret Marchioness of Carnarvon, who was responsible for the new building of Avington church (H), died before she could see the completion of her building project. Her pink and white marble monument stands against the north wall, inside the communion rail. Also commemorated in the church is John Shelley (d.1866), the poet's brother, who had acquired the estate a few years before.

Petersfield (H) has a number of 18th-century monuments to members of the

Lewes, St Anne, iron 'bedhead' memorials in graveyard, 19th-century

Piddinghoe, St John, small iron grave-marker

Jolliffe family, but perhaps most interesting is that to John Sainsbury by Flaxman (1801).

This is not the place for an excursus on churchyard monuments, but one particular type may be mentioned, because it is associated with local materials, trades and craftsmen, as opposed to the grand London designers and imported stone of the gentry monuments in church. This is the so-called 'bedhead' type of memorial, effectively a board supported on two posts, clear of the ground, and furnished with an inscription. The board is usually oriented, that is it runs east to west along the length of the grave, so it is not a headstone. Topographical drawings of the 18th century show that these were very popular at that time, and many were produced by and for the ironmasters of the Weald. They continued into the 19th century, as a cluster of examples at St Anne's, Lewes (ESx), shows. Many must have been made of wood and have not survived, but there is one north of the tower of Ringmer church (ESx), commemorating a miller, who died in 1798.

Twentieth-century memorials include gravestones by Eric Gill at Ditchling (ESx), where he lived and set up a craftsmen's guild, a sundial in the churchyard commemorating the coronation of King George V, and the war memorial on the green just outside the churchyard; there is another at South Harting (WSx), and at Amberley (WSx), where there is a monument by Lutyens in the churchyard. At Liss St Mary (H) there is a carving of the Christ Child, also by Gill. At Westdean (ESx) there are 1950s bronze heads of Oswald Birley and Lord Waverley by Clare Sheridan and Jacob Epstein respectively.

SELECTED CHURCHES

Grotesque head from Poynings, Holy Trinity, N transept E window, early 15th-century, © Roger Rosewell

Avington, St Mary

A church was recorded here in Domesday Book (1086), but the present building is a rare example of a church newly built in the 18th century (it was begun in 1768) in the then fashionable style of the Renaissance. The building material – brick – was also fashionable at the time. In accordance with the prevailing 'Low Church' principles there is no separate chancel to house the altar, so that the body of the church is effectively a rectangular box. The windows are large and plain, with semi-circular heads, except for the E window, which is Venetian, that is a three-light group of which the central light is taller than those flanking it and has a semi-circular head, which they do not. In all these respects the church contrasts with its medieval predecessors, which were usually stone-built and consisted of a nave and chancel, often with one or more side aisles, and had either small splayed windows or larger ones subdivided by stone mullions and tracery.

The furnishings of the church are typical of their period, and were fortunately not affected by the zeal of the 19th-century restorers. The interior is filled with box pews with high panelling, which gave a degree of privacy and kept out the draughts; inside the squire's pew the panels are decorated with carving. Dominating the whole is the three-decker

Interior facing E (see also pp. 9, 56, 57 & 75)

pulpit, both a practical piece of furniture and a symbol of the central importance of the Word of God in 18th-century worship: at the top level were preached the frequently lengthy sermons that were a feature of church (and chapel) services at the time; the middle level was the equivalent of a lectern, from which the Bible readings were pronounced; at the floor level sat the parish clerk, who led the congregation's responses during worship and announced parish business.

At the W end there is a gallery, dated 1771, marking the completion of the church. Here the parish musicians would have led the singing in the fashion described a hundred years later in Thomas Hardy's *Under the Greenwood Tree*; but by Hardy's time the band had been replaced by the present early 19th-century barrel organ in its Gothick-style case, which

is at odds with the rest of the furnishings. At the E end a communion rail of wrought iron (or perhaps lead) divides off the space around the altar, above which, mounted on the end wall is an elaborate panelled reredos bearing the painted Ten Commandments, the Lord's Prayer and the Creed.

Also in the altar area are two monuments; the pink and white marble one on the N wall is to the Countess of Carnarvon, who paid for the building of the church but who died in 1768 before construction was begun. On the S wall of the nave is a Victorian monument, but in the Renaissance style, to John Shelley (†1866), younger brother of the poet Percy Bysshe Shelley, who bought the Avington manor in 1848. It remained in his family until 1951.

Bishop's Waltham, St Peter

St Peter's is one of the earliest Anglo-Saxon minsters in the area and is a building with a well-documented post-Reformation rebuilding history. The earliest mention of Waltham comes in the Life of St Willibald, one of the Anglo-Saxon missionaries to Germany in the 8th century, who received his training at the 'monastery' here. Of the Anglo-Saxon minster church there is no trace, but a piece of a stone cross-shaft of that period has been discovered and is currently (2016) on loan to the Winchester City Museum. Carved

General view from SE (further illustrations on pp. 58 & 75)

stonework of this sort is usually regarded as evidence for a high-status church. In St Willibald's day the great estate which became the Hundred of Waltham was owned by the king, but was later exchanged for a property belonging to the Bishop of Winchester. The bishops henceforth held the estate and the town of Waltham itself, which explains the 'Bishop's' in the present-day name, along with the patronage of St Peter's.

Domesday Book records two churches here, one of which must have been St Peter's. At the time substantial Romanesque churches were tending to replace old Anglo-Saxon minsters, but far-reaching rebuilding has subsequently destroyed much of the evidence for a church of 11th- to 12th-century date at Waltham. At best there are fragments of architectural carved stone dating from the late 12th century. If the present plan of the church represents the Romanesque footprint, then it was indeed a substantial building. In the extant

fabric the earliest survival is the N arcade of the nave, which has slightly double-chamfered arches of around 1200 on piers and capitals of the 1890s. The architectural fragments may have come from the S arcade, which had suffered significant damage in earlier building campaigns and was rebuilt in the 1890s after the fashion of the N arcade; the chancel arch dates from the same campaign. The chancel itself appears to be 15th-century, with traceried windows in the E and side walls, but blocked windows found in the N wall in 1868 suggest a 13th-century origin.

In the post-medieval centuries there were significant alterations, all in a manner known as Gothic Survival, a sort of watered-down version of Perpendicular. The SW tower fell in 1582 and was rebuilt 1584–89, and is low, massive and with straight-headed 'Tudor' windows. The attached stair turret was continued upwards in the 17th century. Then in 1637 the N aisle was rebuilt – note the dated buttress; in the W wall two tiers of windows, the upper of which indicates that there was a gallery, a very non-medieval feature. The S aisle followed in 1652 (date stone over E window), the nave roof was 'new made' in 1669, and the W end of the nave rebuilt in 1849.

The furnishings include a font, rough and of possibly early Norman date, and the stem of a 12th-century pillar piscina reused as a shaft in a later canopied niche. But most of the interest lies in the post-Reformation period: the pulpit of 1626, panels with strapwork arches, and an elaborate sounding board, probably

original, refitted in the late 19th-century; the communion rail with turned balusters and panelled end posts, not precisely dated, but 17th-century; the W gallery of 1733 has original box pews.

Chalton – see Idsworth

Chilcomb, St Andrew

Chilcomb, the only place in its Hundred mentioned by Domesday Book, was a huge estate almost surrounding the City of Winchester; a large part of the present-day parish has become a suburb of Winchester. A small part, often known as Upper Chilcomb, is still a fairly traditional village in a Downland setting, with its church standing somewhat apart from the settlement, seemingly alone on the hillside. This must be the successor to one of the nine churches recorded for Chilcomb in the Domesday Survey; the others have been

General view from N (further illustrations on pp. 8 & 51)

identified, and spread over the surrounding area.

St Andrew's is a simple flint rubble church consisting of an aisle-less nave and rectangular chancel. It has several features of the Romanesque style, which have led to a date of c.1130–40 being proposed. If that is correct, it must be assumed that the Domesday church was an older Anglo-Saxon one, otherwise it would hardly have been replaced within 50 years or so of the Survey. There is a series of round-headed splayed windows, two very plain doorways (that on the N side blocked, apparently with bricks) and a chancel arch without any mouldings; the imposts of the arch are plain chamfered and have typical zigzag decoration on their long vertical faces. The screen may be 17th-century. In the chancel is a pillar piscina with a head in the form of a capital carved with broad leaves of almost waterleaf form; this suggests a date in the second half of the 12th century or possibly even as early as the church itself. In the chancel floor are fifteenth-century glazed tiles with impressed slip patterns, including lions, griffins, eagles, and fleurs-de-lis.

At the W end there is a square weather-boarded turret not sitting on the W gable, which is gently hipped. It is supported on timbers inside the church, which give the roof structure a rather complicated appearance. In the E wall of the nave, above the chancel arch and just visible through the roof timbers internally, are two openings with pointed heads, possibly intended originally to house bells.

Clanfield, St James

There was a chapel here at least since the 13th century, but nothing survives of this in the present building of 1875, except for two medieval bells in the turret and the 14th-century font. It has been claimed that the W window was reused from the old church, but if so it has been heavily renewed. The bell-cote with its two gables forms a significant feature

Richard Ubsdell's painting of Clanfield medieval church, 1841, ref. no. 1945_419_12 (reproduced by kind permission of Portsmouth Museums Service, Portsmouth City Council)

at the W end. The nave and chancel are built of flint, but faced with brick internally, several different colours being used in horizontal bands. Apart from the W window, lancets are used throughout, with three of equal height in the E wall of the chancel.

The traceried chancel screen and communion rail are both of iron.

Corhampton
no known dedication

The church stands high on a knoll at the junction of the roads to West Meon and Bishop's Waltham; the ground falls away precipitously to the dwellings to the N and the road to the E. The church was recorded in Domesday Book and to judge from its

Nave, porch and bell turret from SE

General view from SW (see also p. 35)

Interior facing E

architectural features had stood here since the later Anglo-Saxon period. The nave and part of the chancel survives – the E end was rebuilt in brick in 1855. The angles of the nave are constructed in the manner typical of many late Anglo-Saxon churches, the so-called long-and-short work, in which tall stones alternate with shorter flat stones. The purpose of the flat stones is to bond into the walls to hold the corner together; in some cases the flat stones are broad enough to bond into both walls simultaneously, but more frequently – as here at Corhampton – they are oblong stones which penetrate the fabric of only one of the walls, alternating left and right up the height of the quoin.

Another late Anglo-Saxon characteristic is the pattern of vertical stone strips, known as pilaster strips, which stand proud of the wall surface by about 50mm (2 in.). They are made of dressed stone, which contrasts strongly with the flint rubble of which the walls are built. Similar pilaster strips can be seen at Woolbeding (WSx; see below), but those at Corhampton are rather more sophisticated. Each strip has its own base standing on the plinth of the building, and these simple rectangular blocks are decorated with a series of plain spearhead-shaped leaves. The blocked N door, fairly tall and narrow in the Anglo-Saxon style, is framed by similar strips; on either side the vertical pilasters have moulded imposts, above which the strip follows the semi-circular line of the door head. Inside the church the chancel arch was similarly treated, but the vertical pilasters have been hacked back, leaving only the hood-mould around

Anglo-Saxon sundial

the arch head as a projecting feature. This archway is built of stones which run through the complete thickness of the wall ('through-stones'); in the jambs they are laid alternately flat and on edge, echoing the long-and-short technique of the quoins.

In the nave S wall, to the E of the porch, is an Anglo-Saxon sundial. There are similar sundials at St Michael's, Winchester, and Warnford (H; see below); the dial at Bishopstone (ESx) is of completely different design (see below). In the church is an unusual font, either of Anglo-Saxon or of Norman date, circular, and with a bold rope moulding round its girth.

As though all these early features were not enough, the 12th century adds to the *embarras de richesses*, for in the chancel are substantial remains of wall paintings, restored in 1968 and dated probably around 1125–75. In typical medieval fashion the decoration is arranged in two tiers: the lower represents stylised drapery with square and circular motifs and birds back-to-back in the circles, while there are figural scenes above relating to the Life and Miracles of St Swithun.

In the body of the church are a kingpost roof of *c*.1600 and a simple W gallery.

Droxford, St Mary and All Saints

Droxford is one of a number of settlements in the Meon Valley and was a place of some importance. It is well known to archaeologists as the name of an important Anglo-Saxon cemetery in the centuries preceding the conversion to Christianity, though the site actually lies in Soberton parish. At Domesday (1086) Droxford was the principal place in the

General view from SW

Interior chancel S wall with remains of earlier windows

Corbel head supporting arch

hundred of the same name, and had its own church.

Whether any of the late 11th-century church survives is unclear. The nave and chancel date from the Norman period; the best evidence is the fragmentary remains of two round-headed splayed windows in the S chancel wall, later filled in and partly destroyed by the insertion of the arch into the SE-chapel, but it is not possible to assign a precise date. Two Romanesque doorways survive, reset in the N and S aisle walls. The one on the N side is very weathered, but they appear to be a pair, with much zigzag and saw-tooth decoration, pendant triangle in the hood mouldings and an inner roll moulding with spiralling pelleted strap decoration. This all implies a 12th- rather than an 11th-century date. The chancel arch, with its finer roll moulding and nook shafts could be earlier, however. Aisles were added around 1200; judging by the nave arcades the N aisle was built before the S. There is no

clerestory range of windows, and the roof of the body of the church covers nave and aisles in one sweep, broken only by two dormers on the S slope – the so-called cat-slide roof common in neighbouring Sussex. The chancel, however, has a clerestory and a roof of much shallower pitch with a coved cornice and projecting eaves, which is like 18th-century domestic architecture in the area.

The chapel on the N side of the chancel appears to have been added at the same time as the N aisle; that on the S is later on the evidence of the windows and the detailing of the arch in the chancel S wall, which is supported not on conventional capitals but on human busts in the style of the 14th century. The W tower dates from 1599.

In the nave N wall, adjacent to the chancel arch is the upper doorway of the stairway access to the medieval rood loft, a feature rarely represented in this selection of churches. The side chapels retain their medieval piscinas.

In the S chapels there is a 13th-century carved stone effigy of a lady. From the post-Reformation period there is the communion rail in the chancel: a heavily moulded top rail supported on turned balusters, and with panelled end posts with elegant finials. This is similar to the communion rail at Bishop's Waltham.

East Meon, All Saints

An imposing church, seen from the village with the Downs rising directly behind it. The central tower, with its Romanesque arches and later spire, was the pivotal feature of the original building; the nave, chancel and transepts abutted it, forming the shape of the cross on the ground. There were no aisles; the S aisle was added later – see the obvious straight joint between it and the nave on the W front (helpfully picked out in brick), the difference in style between the arches of the S arcade and the tower arch, and the remains of a round-headed window above the S arcade, which indicate this was once the outside wall of the church.

So the church in the Norman period was what is technically known as an aisle-less cruciform building. This is one of the recognised forms for a high-status church, a mother church with a family of dependent chapels, often the successor of an Anglo-Saxon minster or regional church. East Meon was the sole manor in its Domesday hundred, which included Langrish (an independent parish since 1871) and probably Froxfield and Steep

Nave interior facing E (further illustrations on pp. 22, 38, 46, 56 & 59))

with Ambersham (the latter now in West Sussex), which both have their own churches; there were also chapels at Westbury, St Mary in the Fields and possibly Bereleigh. Before the Norman Conquest All Saints' will have been the hundredal minster, responsible for all of these. This is a measure of its historical importance and the reason for the scale, form and decorative treatment of the Romanesque church.

The central tower is faced with high-quality masonry, imported from Quarr in the Isle of Wight, rather than the flint and other rubble commonly used in the area of the Park, with arris rolls at the exterior angles and three belfry lights to each face with scallop capitals and zigzag decoration. Internally, the arches joining the tower to the nave and chancel also have scallop caps and zigzag mouldings. The W door to the church, originally the ceremonial entrance, is similarly enriched (Quarr stone again). The 12th-century building was a

Heraldic graffiti on stone pier

high-class job, and had a no doubt expensive imported font, made of so-called 'marble' (in reality a highly polished dark limestone) from Tournai in Belgium; two faces are decorated with blind arcading and plant scroll with animals, while the other two are pictorial, showing scenes from the story of Adam and Eve. Tournai fonts are rare, and occur elsewhere in Hampshire only in Winchester Cathedral, St Michael's Southampton, and St Peter's at St Mary Bourne.

This splendid Romanesque church was extended in the 13th century by the addition of the S aisle and Lady Chapel, and re-modelled at the E end in the 15th by Prior

Hinton of Winchester Cathedral Priory whose arms are carved on the exterior of the new E wall of the chancel. The earlier chancel, from the Norman period, must have been slightly out of alignment, judging from the remnant of its lower walling still visible on the N side. The great E window in the Perpendicular style was designed by Sir Ninian Comper in the first half of the 20th century; the glass constitutes a memorial to the allies who fought the First World War. Comper also designed the altar and its furnishings, and the screen between the chancel and the Lady Chapel to its south.

Finally, as you leave the church you will see above the S door a painted Royal Arms. This is dated 1613 and is a rare example of the arms of James I, whose initials – I and R, for Iacobus Rex – can just be seen on the extreme left- and right-hand sides of the composition.

Easton, St Mary

Easton belonged to the bishops of Winchester, who had two small churches or chapels here in 1086. Whether either of these stood on the site of the present parish church is not known. St Mary's has a striking appearance: at the W end a tall stair turret attached to the tower and at roof level has a gallery-like projection linking it to the nave roof; at the E end the chancel with its apse looks very massive and might be taken for part of a castle building. The reason for this heavy build can be seen inside the church: the chancel and the apse each has a rib vault, that is a stone ceiling supported on

ribs of stone with decorative carving. These vaults exert outward pressure on the walls, which are massively built to resist this. As it is, it can be seen that the arches between the chancel and the apse and between the nave and the chancel have spread, so that their jambs are no longer vertical. The details of this work suggest a date between about 1175 and 1200. Apparently of the same date is the elaborately decorated S nave door, but much of the work is the result of the restoration in the 1860s; in the equivalent position in the N wall the doorway is very plain, and blocked. There are two Romanesque splayed windows in the N wall of the nave. There were presumably similar windows on the S side,

General view from S (see also p. 53)

but they were replaced in the 15th century by square-headed two-light windows.

Inside the nave at the W end there is a round-headed doorway high above the tower arch. The arch at ground floor level is pointed, that is looking forward to the new Gothic style of the 13th century and later. The high doorway, however, still has a semi-circular head in the 'old' Romanesque style. It was not intended to be seen by the public, and in such positions old-fashioned features were often employed, possibly using up a stock of stones already cut to shape or working with existing timber centring to form the arch. Doorways in this position were common from the 11th to the 13th century, and led from the tower to an attic above the nave, with a floor of boards laid on the tie-beams of the roof; it is known that such spaces in churches were used in the Middle Ages for storage. In these cases the congregation in the nave would have seen a flat ceiling above them, not the open timber roof that exists today.

Chancel viewed through chancel arch

In the NE corner of the nave are two doorways, one above the other, connected by a staircase housed in a projecting turret, which can be seen on the outside. Before the Reformation this stair was used to gain access to the rood loft, a gallery on a beam across the church where the great crucifix (rood) stood or hung. Here candles were lit in honour of the crucified Christ, the vestments of the rood figures were changed according to the ecclesiastical season, sermons could be preached and the parish chest was kept: parishioners could have their valuables looked after in an early form of village safe deposit. The other liturgical fittings of the church are modern, with the exception of the trefoil piscina in the chancel and the Jacobean pulpit, which has arched panels at the base and arabesque panels above.

There is a monument of historical interest to the wife of an early Anglican bishop: he had been a monk (and therefore celibate) in the days before the Reformation.

Hambledon, St Peter and St Paul

'A large and complex building, almost like a text-book of medieval parish church architecture' (Pevsner). To help understand the complexities there is a copy of an architect's plan on display in the church and reproduced in the *Little Handbook* available there (and see above, p. 24).

The core of the church is an Anglo-Saxon nave and chancel, but despite the probable

General view from NW (see p. 24 for plan)

existence of a church here in 1086, there is no mention of it in Domesday Book. The evidence for the Anglo-Saxon fabric can be seen in the walls of the outer and inner naves as viewed from the side aisles. As is usually the case, these aisles are later additions, so what can be seen from them are the original outside walls of the early church. In the outer nave there are substantial remains of pilaster strips, of the sort prominent in the fabric of Corhampton, less than five miles away. Here they have been cut away by the insertion of the arcade arches. On the N side of the inner nave there is a horizontal moulding or string course, which projects slightly from the wall surface. This starts at the W end of the wall but stops short roughly halfway along it: this shows the original extent of the chancel wall of the first church, which was narrower than the nave. This chancel was lengthened later on, then superseded by the present chancel, at which point it was incorporated into the nave. This explains why the present outer

nave is wider than the inner nave (as is the new chancel). Between the two there remains the chancel arch of the extended chancel; this had replaced the Anglo-Saxon arch, and dates from the early 13th century – the pointed arch, mouldings and engaged shaft are the evidence for that.

Aisles appear to have been added to the original ('outer') nave in the later 12th century; there are small Romanesque windows in the aisle W walls, the one on the N side having apparently been moved outwards, implying the widening of an existing narrower aisle. The other aisle windows are of later date. The arches leading into these aisles can be dated to the 1180s on the N side (round pier, scallop capitals with square abaci, slightly pointed arches) and slightly later on the S (slenderer piers, round capitals and abaci, double-chamfered arches, fully developed dogtooth ornament). There is comparable, though not identical, evidence for the aisles of the early chancel ('inner' nave): first comes the very plain pointed arch beneath the Anglo-Saxon string course, so perhaps the first addition was simply a side chapel or vestry; then the extended N wall has an arcade of two bays with double-chamfered arches and plain round piers, indicating that the side chapel was extended E to form an aisle; finally the S arcade of three bays with octagonal piers and capitals and double-chamfered arches, leading to a S aisle. Externally these aisles have lancet side windows, later replaced by three-light Perpendicular windows; in the E wall of the N aisle three lancet-shaped lights, with a foiled circle above, all below a super-arch; a similar embracing arch on the S side, but with 19th-century graded lights.

The present chancel dates from the 13th century and has a trefoil piscina with a small projecting basin, paired lancets in the side walls and a Victorian replacement E window. The side walls were heightened in the later Middle Ages to accommodate a low-pitched roof, typical of the period, panelled internally. The remaining roofs are of steeper pitch and earlier: tree-ring analysis of the timbers gives dates of 1348–80 for the inner nave and its N aisle, and 1445–77 for the outer nave. Other late medieval developments were the addition of a two-storeyed Perpendicular-style S porch and a two-storeyed vestry S of the tower (both upper floors have been removed). The tower had been built in the 13th century, but was rebuilt after a fire in 1794 with mixed rubble of flint and small stone blocks and brick dressings.

The individuality of this remarkable building has been enhanced in more recent times by regimental 'colours' (flags) of the Hambledon Volunteers (pre-1810); fine hangings at the W end (later 19th-century, to a design by William Morris); a modern (1953) royal coat of arms; and the eye-catching, if not garish, chancel ceiling installed by the church architect Stephen Dykes Bower, who was Surveyor to the Fabric of Westminster Abbey in the 1960s.

Idsworth, St Hubert (RM-G)
(see illustrations on pp. 7 & 63 and on the rear cover)

Idsworth Church, nowadays improbably – and (as we shall see) fancifully – dedicated to St Hubert, is astonishing in several different respects. It is surprisingly, but beautifully, set on an empty hillside in an out-of-the-way location on the Hants–W Sussex border, with no dwelling nearby: its village long deserted, even the manor house abandoned when the London-Portsmouth railway was pushed through the lonely valley beneath.

It looks like the quintessential small Downland church (see back cover). The nave quoins and a narrow, blocked N doorway and small window are typically early-Norman (even if the church was founded by Earl Godwin just before the Conquest). There is a quirky bell turret and a charming W porch. Inside, the impression is of a consistently maintained 18th-century building: good box pews and pulpit, 'churchwarden' windows with wooden tracery, a W gallery (now housing an organ). A late 18th-century plan showing the disposition of the then current congregation among the pews is on display.

A slightly pointed chancel arch is unexpectedly surmounted by a panel with a painting (in fresco technique) of Christ in Majesty by the contemporary artist Fleur Kelly: a millennial project (2000), containing a host of references – both general and specific to Idsworth. Older

paintings await us beyond the arch, however, and they are Idsworth's most remarkable feature.

Much of the chancel N wall is taken up by two tiers of comparatively well-preserved painting with a chevron band in between, probably dating from the early 14th century. This was discovered under limewash in 1864, and from the start caused lively debate. The lower tier illustrates, with expressionistic contortions, episodes from the life of John the Baptist: largely the feast of Herod, in which Salome dances to Herod's pleasure and her mother Herodias demands the Baptist's head. Above is an apparent hunting scene, with a pack of dogs

Painted figure of St Paul on splay of E window

and a strange shaggy beast with a human face. Current opinion inclines to interpret this as a 'hairy anchorite', in one or another version of an extravagant late-medieval legend involving his sin and ultimate salvation. Earlier, though, it was thought to represent the life of St Hubert: hence the curious rededication of the church, c.1900.

The connection between the upper and lower tiers has been variously and ingeniously interpreted. But is it even necessary to establish a relationship? The problem, as so often, is that we have only a fragment of the cycle or cycles, vivid as these portions are; if we knew what had been represented on the adjoining walls, even on the rest of the N. wall, things might more easily fall into place. Meanwhile we should not overlook the distinguished, if faded representations on the splays of the E. window showing St Peter and St Paul (no doubt the original dedicatees) within architectural settings.

The chancel N. wall scenes too have faded somewhat since their discovery (maybe thanks to Tristram's deleterious restoration methods), but a drawing displayed underneath helps to clarify them. There is a well-preserved graffito of 15th-century character visible as well. The entire church has been beautifully maintained, and is a singular pleasure to visit.

St Hubert's was originally a chapelry of **CHALTON**, an important settlement in the early Middle Ages from which the Hundred took its name. There the church of St Michael has an E window of four lights with foiled circles above,

an example of the Geometrical style of Early English tracery, which is a rarity in this area.

Itchen Stoke
[Churches Conservation Trust]
and Itchen Abbas

Two interesting but contrasting mid-Victorian churches in adjacent villages. Itchen Abbas, St John the Baptist, retains a genuine early Romanesque doorway with shafts, cushion

Itchen Abbas: Romanesque doorcase reused in the porch (see also p. 19)

Itchen Stoke: lectern and decorative ironwork panels of pulpit

capitals and billet ornament, reset in the porch. The remainder of the church is of 1867 (chancel) and 1883 (nave and transeptal space) in the neo-Norman style. The chancel arch and the E window pick up motifs from the porch door, with convincing-looking billet ornament, while the remainder of the church is a plainer sort of neo-Romanesque. New churches in this style were less common in the Victorian period than various forms of neo-Gothic, so that St John's makes an interesting contrast

Itchen Stoke: general view from SW (see p. 19)

with neighbouring St Mary's in Itchen Stoke, which was an almost exact contemporary.

Built in 1866, St Mary's, Itchen Stoke, is regarded as a remarkable example of Gothic Revival architecture. It is tall, with a steep roof and a bell-cote at the E end. The windows in the side walls are lancets of Early English type. There is a wheel window in the W wall and the rather complex apse has windows with bar tracery. Inside, the apse is vaulted; the W wall has blind arcading and the window reveals are shafted.

The font is adorned with coloured enamel, gilt bronze and black marble; the pulpit and bench-ends have inset cast-iron panels; the apse floor has a maze pattern.

The building was paid for by the then incumbent and designed by his brother Henry Conybeare, who is said to have been inspired by the Sainte Chapelle in Paris.

Liss, St Mary – *see Privett*

Meonstoke, St Andrew

At Domesday (1086) the bishop of Winchester held half a hide in this manor and had 20 shillings from the church of Meonstoke. There is no evidence of this early date in the present fabric of St Andrew's, however, which appears to be in the Early English and later styles. The tower and the chancel both have lancet windows of 13th-century date, and the nave arcades have alternating piers of round and octagonal shape supporting double-chamfered arches. Above the arcades in the relatively low nave walls are quatrefoiled circular clerestory windows, now visible only inside the church. The outer reveals must have been external originally, looking out on to the formerly saddleback roofs of the aisles, for which the supporting corbels can still be

Nave interior facing E (see also p. 48)

Painted dedication cross in chancel

seen in the side walls. An earlier nave roof can be deduced from the inverted-V weathering on the W wall of the nave; this was replaced, probably in the early 17th century, by a wagon roof, the curved line of which can just be made out below the weathering. This roof destroyed the lower half of the weathering and of the round-headed window that went

General view from SE

with it; the window was replaced at a slightly lower level. The present roof is a cat-slide covering both nave and side aisles. The timber superstructure of the tower was added 1899-1902.

Late 14th-century work in the chancel has been associated with the gift of the church to Winchester College in 1384. The E window, flanked by ornate niches originally intended for statues, is in the style of William Wynford, the master mason who designed and built the College. Judging by the set-back in the wall above the window, the late medieval chancel had a low-pitched roof typical of that period. Also of the 14th century a low tomb recess in the N wall. Above this, between the windows, a painted dedication cross, the date of which is not known.

The square font of Purbeck marble has a very shallow top element with flat round-headed arcading in relief; it is the earliest feature of the church. The hexagonal pulpit dates from the 17th century, but has modern carved panels; the corner supports in the form of detached barley-sugar twists are original.

Newton Valence – *see Selborne*

Petersfield, St Peter

St Peter's stands to the south of the now pedestrianized market place. It is scarcely credible that this large and magnificent

Interior of nave facing E (further illustrations on pp. 25 & 38)

church was until 1886 a mere chapelry of Mapledurham (now the village of Buriton), despite an attempt in 1657–58 to establish Petersfield as a separate parish. This is an example of the not uncommon feature of role reversal, whereby a dependency overtakes the mother church in importance and prestige. This appears to have been happening already in the late 12th century, when a papal document mistakenly refers to the 'church of Petersfield and the chapel of Mapledurham'. In 1265 it was agreed that tithes due to Mapledurham should be paid in the 'great church' of Petersfield (*in majori ecclesia de Peteresfeld*).

The surviving parts of the Romanesque building, though it has been much rebuilt, are impressive and justify the description 'great church'. Its building history is extremely complicated. Inside the nave, the elevation of the E end is unusually tall and elaborate, with arched openings at different levels; the

explanation for this is that we are not looking at a conventional chancel arch wall, but the interior of the E wall of a central tower, the other three walls of which have been removed, while the later nave arcades were continued through the central space to abut the surviving E wall. The lower parts of the side (N and S) walls were not entirely removed, however; in the angles where the arcades abut the E wall, remains of the original tower arches can be seen. The responds (the end supports) of the N and S tower arches were retained; they match those of the chancel arch, with shafts and volute capitals and fragments of the hood mould with billet ornament. This is quite different from the nave arcades, which have solid circular piers and circular capitals with scallop or leaf decoration and plain arches. So the nave and its side aisles cannot have been built until the original central

Richard Ubsdell's painting of Petersfield church before restoration, 1846, ref. no. 1945_419_46 (reproduced by kind permission of Portsmouth Museums Service, Portsmouth City Council) (compare pp. 15 & 26)

tower was partly demolished, for whatever reason. It has been suggested that the tower was never completed, but initially this seems unlikely, given that the transepts were built to the N and S of it. Their end walls survive at the E ends of the side aisles – the parts without a string course below the windows, with fabric including herringbone masonry – though there is no guarantee that they were carried up to full height; it may be that the remodeling of the church took place before the crossing and transepts were finished. If that were the case, some imagination is

required to see how the church was used between the building of the eastern parts in the earlier 12th century and the construction of the nave and aisles towards the end of the century.

The late Romanesque work included the addition of a W tower, whose doorway to the exterior has shafted jambs; on the S side one of the shafts has a waterleaf capital, which serves to date the work to the last third of the 12th century. Inside the church, the E wall of the tower has a projecting weathering in the form of an inverted V, which covered the end of the original nave roof. At the time there was no clerestory; the present one was built by Sir Arthur Blomfield, the architect of the far-reaching restoration of 1873-74. The N porch was built about 10 years later, and partly covers one of the original windows of the N aisle, below which there is fabric evidence for a disused doorway.

Petersfield, St Laurence
(Roman Catholic)

On Station Road, a little below the level crossing a large handsome church of Italianate type: cruciform, with aisle-less nave, chancel and transepts all abutting a central space surmounted by an octagonal lantern drum and dome. The use of dark red brick is un-Italian. Internally the nave has a segmental vault; the interior is plain and tranquil; Stations of the Cross from Oberammergau.

Font

General view of St Laurence (RC)

Interior of St Laurence (RC)

At Bowyers Common, Steep, NW of Petersfield, the former **Primitive Methodist chapel** is a simple rectangular building of 1869 with round-headed windows and entrance door.

An utterly surprising church to find in a rural location; one of the most imposing Victorian churches in the Park, rivalled only by Arundel Cathedral. It was designed by Sir Arthur Blomfield, (who did much work in the area, building Liss St Mary and restoring Petersfield and Newton Valence; see above and below), and built in 1876–78. It is big and bold, with a tall W tower and broach spire, built of whole flints and much squared Bath and Ham Hill stone. The nave has four-bay arcades with impressive arches leading into N and S aisles and a range of clerestory windows above; the chancel is flanked by transeptal chapels. The E window is of three graded lancets above blind arcading which includes figure sculpture; in the S wall sedilia and a piscina – all of these with dark marble shafting. At the W end there is a very tall tower arch.

There is a great deal of stone sculpture, not only in the reredos below the E window, already mentioned. Many of the minor capitals, for example the chancel arch, inside the church have rich leaf decoration; so have the capitals of the belfry lights externally, and

General view from NE

Interior facing NW

above them there are sprays of leaves in the spandrels of the arches. There is similar leaf decoration on the font. There is also figure carving on the exterior, for example Christ the King above the porch entrance. Stone – in this case Italian marble – is also used for the decorative flooring.

In addition to the font, the furnishings include a stone pulpit and an elaborately decorated wrought iron reading desk.

Until 1874 Privett was a chapelry of West Meon, first mentioned in 1391. By the mid-16th century at the latest it had burial rights. The present church replaced an earlier one,

Anonymous watercolour of the earlier church from the Hampshire Churches albums, HC 413 (© The Dean & Chapter of Winchester 2015; Reproduced by kind permission of the Dean & Chapter of Winchester)

built – or added to – in 1834, and was paid for out of the profits of gin production.

Blomfield also built the church of St Mary, **LISS**, in 1891–92. It is less exciting than Privett, but worth a visit to see the small sculpture of the child Christ by Eric Gill (see Ditchling, WSx). There is now a replica in its original position above the porch entrance; the original is inside the church.

Selborne and Newton Valence

Selborne, St Mary

Across the village green from Gilbert White's house, the church stands in a large and attractive churchyard with ancient trees. Much of the medieval building was altered in 1856 by William White, Gilbert's great-nephew, but the nave arcades – described by Pevsner as 'impressive' – survive. They are important in showing the transition from

Selborne church from S (further illustrations pp. 42 & 43)

Tower of Newton Valence church (see also p. 51)

Romanesque to early Gothic: the piers are circular and carry multi-scalloped capitals with square abaci above, hallmarks of Romanesque style, but the arches are pointed and without embellishment, characteristic of the Early English version of the Gothic style. In other churches and in other parts of the country different forms of this transition can be found, for example Gothic piers still bearing semi-circular arches – and note the doorways in

the W wall of Easton St Mary (H; see above), the lower one pointed and the upper round-headed. Any number of combinations and permutations can be found in the period c.1180 to c.1220.

What the church was like before this is not known, but it was already in existence in 1086. Its later development is complex, not least because of a series of rebuildings and restorations in the 18th and 19th centuries. The tower, for example, exhibits features of a number of different styles and bears a date stone 1781. The S aisle had already been widened some time after 1234; it is floored with 13th-century tiles, many reclaimed from Selborne Priory.

Selborne, former Congregational chapel

A 'typical village chapel with polygonal masonry facing to walls, brick dressings and slate roof. Gabled front with porch and paired lancets. Built 1860' (as described in 1967).

Newton Valence, St Mary

A narrow lane leads from Selborne to the isolated village of Newton. It is worth visiting to see what a church built fully in the Early English style is like. It has the characteristic lancet windows – tall and narrow with pointed heads, and a wide splay to the interior. The S window of the nave is of this type and so are several in the chancel; the group of three in the E wall, the one in the centre higher than the others, is an arrangement often to be seen in chancels that were not updated later in the medieval period. The three windows are closely spaced and represent a point in the development from a single or two widely spaced E windows (see Greatham, WSx, below) to the larger mullioned 'picture' window of the Decorated and Perpendicular periods.

There is one lancet in the W wall of the tower, but the door below is an insertion in the Perpendicular style, and the brick top dates from 1812. The Early English style is represented elsewhere by the priest's door in the S wall of the chancel; inside the chancel on the same wall is a piscina, its pointed head cusped to form a three-lobed pattern (a trefoil). It incorporates the shaft and head of a pillar piscina of 12th-century type, which was originally intended to be free-standing. There is a reredos of *c.*1500 with three recesses, from which the original statues are missing.

Soberton, Sts Peter and Paul

Considering that until the late 19th century it was a mere chapelry of Meonstoke, St Peter's is an unexpectedly large and structurally complex church with impressive remains of an elaborate scheme of decoration in the S transept. Equally noteworthy are the inscriptions on two of the bells, which imply a pre-Reformation date and suggest that the prerogative of using bells, usually restricted to parish churches, was granted at an early stage; quasi-parochial status must be assumed.

The earliest evidence, only visible inside the W tower, consists of the heads of two windows,

Interior facing W (further illustrations on pp. 45, 49 & 74)

which appear to belong to an aisle-less nave and chancel of Romanesque date. A N arcade of two arches was inserted later in the 12th century when the N aisle was added, but this appears to have been shorter than the nave, leaving the western part of the N wall intact. The central support of the arcade is circular, with a square abacus. In the early 13th century an equally short arcade was inserted on the S side with octagonal piers and capitals. Later in the 13th century the arcades were continued W by the addition of a normal-width and a narrow arch on either side. Of the same broad date, the chancel arch with shaft bases set at an extraordinary high level, perhaps because

there was a solid stone screen below. But most striking is the S transept, which has a suite of two windows in the E wall with an altar reredos recess between them. The windows are trefoil-headed externally and cinquefoil internally; the recess has a simple pointed head with plain bar tracery set in it. The back of the recess and the splays of the windows are painted with figures of female saints, which survive from *c.*1300; in the N window St Anne with the young St Mary, and in the S window St Margaret and an unidentified figure. The image in the recess is practically

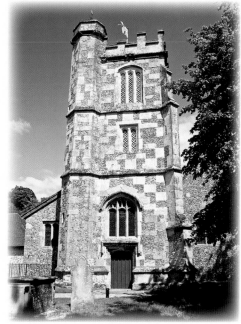

W tower

unrecognisable, but is presumably St Mary the Virgin. The figures are set against a painted representation of masonry, with red joints between rectangular 'blocks', each with one or two stencilled rosettes. This pattern covers much of the E wall of the transept and there is also a strip of it above the arch into the nave. At the top of E transept wall is a painted frieze with a delicate running scroll.

The W end of the church is puzzling. Internally there are blind arches flanking the tower arch, and on the exterior (that is, in the base of the present tower) the springings of two arches running E–W. It has been suggested that these arches supported an earlier, narrower tower, through which there was a N–S passageway. The church plan (copy on display) shows the blind arches as open on either side of the arch from the tower into the nave, and it is difficult to understand how this all worked. Perhaps rather than a narrow tower there was some sort of broad narthex, which was rationalized into the more conventional tower that still exists. At all events, the present tower appears to date from the early 16th century since its openings, particularly the belfry lights, are of the reduced form of Gothic which became common at or after the Reformation.

Warnford, Our Lady

A church is mentioned at one of the Warnford manors in the Domesday Book entry (1086). It is possible that the remains excavated in the course of the 1906 restoration represent the nave of that church. The N and S walls were

followed for about 40 feet (12m) without finding the E end. The W end appears to be represented by vertical lines of squared stone in the W wall of the present nave, flanking the tower arch. The stout Romanesque tower seems to have been built up against this early church, which was then replaced by the existing building. These two events are normally ascribed to the lord of the manor whose tenure ran from 1171 until 1213; this

General view from S (see also p. 75)

Inscription and sundial in S porch

was Adam de Port, successor of Hugh, who held the manor at Domesday. The tower can be dated to the early part of his tenure, and the nave and chancel to near the end. The restoration architect published a drawing showing a weathering on the W wall of the nave, which indicates a building with lower side walls and a steeply pitched roof.

Adam's restoration of the church is recorded in a Latin inscription on the outside wall of the church, inside the porch. A matching inscription in the N wall, above the position of the former N door, names the founder of the church as Wulfric (*not* St Wilfrid, as is commonly claimed). He is likely to be the same as the Wulfric who was co-tenant of the manor at Domesday, probably identical with the abbot of the New Minster in Winchester, who was in office 1067–72.

So the earliest surviving fabric is the W tower, 'broad and sturdy' and 'assertively Norman', according to Pevsner; it has heavy clasping buttresses and unusual circular belfry lights. The nave and chancel have lancet windows, and chamfered pointed arches to the doorways; the tower arch is also pointed. An early 13th-century date can be accepted. The E window of three lights has flowing tracery in the Decorated style, dated 1377; what was there before is not known. The window is set in a massive round-headed arch, visible only inside the church; the interpretation of this is uncertain, but it may have been an open arch leading to an apse or a rectangular chancel.

This E end of the church is full of interest. The chancel screen is dated 1634, was repaired in 1906 and the arcading renewed in 1958. The altar rail, which runs right across the chancel, is 18th-century in origin, but the unusual pierced balusters were described in 1908 as 'modern' – presumably part of the 1906 restoration. Inside the enclosed space and against the E wall are two wall monuments. To the left of the E window a modest alabaster piece without figures, just a plain inscription panel. It commemorates William Neale, who acquired the manor in 1577 and died in 1601. On the right-hand side a much more elaborate monument to Sir Thomas Neale (d.1621), with three effigies, a coffered arch and canopy and kneeling children against the tomb chest.

The font is disappointing: table type on five supports, but the carving worn off. Above the inscription panel in the S porch is a stone sundial with leaves filling the spaces in the corners of the square block, similar to the one at Corhampton.

Arundel, Our Lady and St Philip Howard
(Roman Catholic)

Viewed from the south, the Arundel townscape is dominated by the cathedral and the castle. But for the Englishness of the castle, one might be looking at a French town. The cathedral, whose site is said to have been chosen to achieve this dominance, has been described as 'a triumphant recreation of a 13th-century French cathedral'. It was designed in 1868–69 by J A Hansom and built between 1870 and 1873 to celebrate the then Duke of Norfolk's coming of age. The architect is known not only for the design of other Roman Catholic places of worship and for a range of domestic buildings in Arundel, but also for the cab that bears his name. The size and magnificence of the building made it ideally suitable to become the cathedral of the newly instituted Roman Catholic Diocese of Arundel and Brighton in 1965.

The church consists of a nave with side aisles, N and S transepts and an apse with an ambulatory and flanking chapels. There is no central tower, but simply a flèche above the crossing. At the W end is a narthex and baptistery and the substantial substructure for

Interior facing E

Arundel Cathedral towers above the roofs of the town

a tower and spire that were never built. Inside, the church is very high and has stone vaulting. The nave arcades leading into the narrow side aisles are tall and have eight-shafted piers. The plan, details and soaring height are all French characteristics, but in the W portal there are stiff-leaf capitals of Early English type.

The apse windows and the tall lancets in the transept E walls have coloured glass by the well-known firm of Hardman and Co., but the glass in the nave is plain, and contributes to the bareness of the interior. Less plain are the confessionals in the S aisle, which have elaborately crocketed gables, while the S transept altar to St. Philip Neri has a high canopy with a statue of the saint in French Gothic style. In the Lady Chapel a magnificent ormolu tabernacle made in 1730 to the design of James Gibbs, a Scottish Catholic architect.

Arundel, St Nicholas

The building consists of two distinct parts, physically separated by screens. To the W is a nave of five bays with N and S aisles, to the E of which is a crossing tower and transepts. This constitutes the parish church of St Nicholas. To the E of the tower is a long rectangular 'chancel', which performs the function of private mortuary chapel for the Fitzalan-Howard family, successively earls and dukes of Norfolk; to its N is a three-bay Lady Chapel and sacristy. These chapels were once part of the College of the Holy Trinity, founded in 1380 by Richard FitzAlan, 11th Earl of Arundel. They can be entered only from the castle grounds, but it is possible to view the family monuments and chantry chapels through the glass screen that now separates them from the body of the church.

The dedication to St Nicholas is mentioned in Domesday Book, a sign of 'superior' status, and later evidence refers to 'twelve secular canons of the English nation': it had clearly been an Anglo-Saxon minster. The existing church, however, is late-medieval in an area where church development generally seems to come to a halt around 1300. It is apparently a single-period church built in a consistent style, Perpendicular, which is otherwise poorly represented in West Sussex. The shapes of the doorcases and the arcade piers, the window tracery, and the carved stonework – notably the corbels supporting the roof timbers – all point to this. Another late-medieval feature consists of two south-facing doorways, one

General view from SW, showing central tower, S transept, S aisle with nave clerestory above, and the upper walling of the Fitzalan Chapel extreme right (for the interior of the last, see p. 71)

above the other, giving access to and from the rood loft stair built into the NE pier of the crossing tower.

There is a huge amount of reused stonework from an earlier church both in the exterior walls and the adjoining wall of the priory ruins, and a record of 'richly decorated pieces of stone' found in coffins below the Fitzalan chapel. The footprint of the present church hints at the form and date of this earlier church. The transepts project very little beyond the line of the side aisles. It is normal for transepts to measure more N–S than E–W, but here the reverse is the case: their length is only about two-thirds of their width. Shallow transepts often occur in Romanesque cruciform churches which are the successors

of Anglo-Saxon minsters; a good example can be found in SDNP at East Meon (H). It is possible therefore that such a building is embedded in the later fabric of St Nicholas.

Among the furnishings and fittings the pulpit is a rarity; not only is it a Perpendicular-style piece of the late medieval period, when pulpits were as yet uncommon, but it is made of stone, which is rare at any period. The font is also Perpendicular. The original metal grille separating the nave from the Fitzalan Chapel is still in place: another rarity. Much of the interesting furniture is to be found in the Chapel: tombs of the earls and dukes of Norfolk and miniature chantry chapels from the 15th and early 16th centuries; timber bosses from the original roof reused in the present one of 1886; and in the Lady Chapel a few choir stalls. On the N wall of the N aisle a mural painting of the Seven Deadly Sins and the Seven Works of Mercy, late 14th-century, faded almost to monochrome, and around the church six red-painted consecration crosses.

Botolphs, St Botolph's church
[Churches Conservation Trust]

A church was recorded here in Domesday Book, but under the original settlement name of Annington; there are still an Annington House and Annington Farm nearby, and the Down immediately to the W is called Annington Hill. The hamlet later assumed the name of the patron saint of its church, something that is rare in the SE of England, but more common in other parts of the country (St Albans, St Andrews, St Neots …). The dedication to St Botolph is not original, however; it was formerly to St Peter at the Old Bridge. The river crossing here was superseded by Bramber bridge in the late 11th century, and the name seems to have been gradually changed in the 13th and 14th, so the dedication must have changed before that.

General view from SE (see also p. 9)

The basic structure of the church could well date from the time of Domesday Book (1086). The chancel arch has a bold roll moulding under its head, which stops off at corbel-like capitals; this is a feature common to a number of churches often described as 'late Anglo-Saxon' – for example, the tower arch at Sompting (in SDNP; see below) and the chancel arch at Bosham on the WSx coast. It is now thought that these churches may well have been built after the Norman Conquest, but not yet in a fully Romanesque ('Norman') style.

Like most local churches of the period, St Botolph's consisted simply of a nave and chancel, though there might have been small side chambers (perhaps vestries or chapels) which have since disappeared. There is a small 11th-century window in the S wall of the nave, showing that this was an outside wall. In the 13th century the church was extended by the addition of the W tower and a N aisle. The latter was removed at some time after the Reformation, when the need to accommodate the extra altars, for which it had been built, was past. The arcade that led into it is still there, however, visible both outside and inside the church. Externally the blocking is in a totally different fabric from the rest of the nave wall, and internally the chamfered arch heads and the capitals of the arches stand out very clearly.

The furnishings include a Jacobean pulpit, which is a rarity in Sussex, indeed in SDNP as a whole. The sounding board and other surfaces are covered with fine incised abstract patterns. Fragments of early wall paintings survive.

Buncton (RM-G)

All Saints, Buncton, at first sight a humble building of early-Norman origin, is disproportionately interesting, even mysterious. It stands in a striking location opposite Chanctonbury Hill, above a steep little valley, nowadays without a nearby village. Once it overlooked the important E–W Roman road called the 'Greensand Way'. At the time

of Domesday Book (1086) Buncton was a place of significance, with 26 households; but in the late Middle Ages it declined as Ashington – a couple of miles NW – grew. Situated in a detached pocket of Ashington parish (which has a church of 14th- to 15th-century date), it came to be regarded as a chapel of the latter; in recent times it has become part of Wiston, which also has a church of medieval origin, much restored.

Romanesque arcading reused in chancel N wall

The exterior has puzzling aspects, though the characteristically Norman Caen stone quoins and doorways (one blocked) look straightforward enough. The walls turn out to be an amazing hotch-potch of materials, mostly flint, with many Roman brick fragments. The S nave wall, alarmingly bowed, contains much Georgian brick, clearly the result of an urgent repair job ('1758' can be read on an inset stone). Three strange rounded elements are explicable as the ends of cut-off columns laid horizontally. Where

General view from NW

N wall of nave: Procession to the Holy City (see also p. 61)

these could come from is seen when we look at the N of the chancel. The remains of three elaborate late-Norman arches, cut down and appearing pointed, have been applied to the earlier wall with its lancet windows. To the S there are a couple more, simpler, arches. Between them, the chancel E wall presents the surprising spectacle of another batch of Caen stone, of good quality but haphazardly laid, enclosing a fine 14th-century window. The builders seem to have run out of this material before reaching the gable and had to finish off their task with flints. This stone was clearly a job lot, brought from elsewhere – perhaps from Steyning (whose large church underwent significant reduction), more probably from Sele Priory at Beeding, which had a financial crisis *c*.1300, necessitating considerable demolition work.

Inside, the church is dominated by a chancel arch so high that it has been suggested it too underwent 18th-century rebuilding, though it is of Caen stone (not imported after the Middle Ages till modern times). Above it there is a void, suggesting that earlier there was a sleeping-platform. Certainly the villagers could lock themselves in: there are gaps to take a bar on the interior of the doorway. The E wall has pre-Reformation image-brackets on either side of the 14th-century window; there are well-preserved aumbry and piscina. There is a fragment of 14th-century fleur-de-lys painting in the nave, and there is some evidence that more survives under the whitewash. But the strangest and most alluring interior feature survives no longer. This was a small, apparently naked carved figure with a hatched roundel above its head (and more, smaller roundels above that) on the N impost of the arch, together with billet and cable moulding. Figure and roundels were chiselled off in November 2004, and the pieces left on the floor. It had been suggested that the figure had a malign influence, and internet sources are keen to call it a sheela-na-gig of pagan import: but the evidence is strong that the unfortunate (early Romanesque) carving was of our forefather Adam at the moment of his 'enlivenment', or creation.

Clayton, St John the Baptist (RM-G)

Clayton Church, nestled in a small village at the foot of the 'wind gap' – always an important axis of communication – leading to the Brighton/Portslade area, is justly famous

for its beautiful, extensive and very early wall paintings. But even without them it would be a notable building.

A walk round the outside reveals a church that (apart from a small vestry attached to the N) has hardly been affected by modern restoration. Massive quoin stones, particularly impressive to the W, are of pre-Norman character. The walls, of un-coursed flints with remains of old, pinkish render in places, are only 28 inches thick – again, a pre-Norman sign. On both N and S sides, outside and in, fragmentary stonework indicates the one-time existence of arches leading to side chambers – the one on the north may have had the character of a pre-Norman *porticus*; though the arches now appear pointed, this is may be the result of later medieval reconstruction. A plan published in the *Victoria County History* states that these chambers were revealed by excavation in 1918, but no further information is available. The windows, however, betray modernization: the triple E window was put into an earlier aperture in 1838. Lancets of 13th-century character were discovered in the chancel during a refurbishment of the 1980s. It was generally thought the chancel had been lengthened at that time; but remains of wall painting like that in the nave have been uncovered at the E end of its N wall, implying a single build.

General view from S

The church is entered through a medieval wooden door from a porch reconstructed of old materials. The nave is impressive not through grand dimensions, but for its height and particularly for the noble chancel arch, its emphatic triple roll-moulding scarcely interrupted by plain imposts – it seems to stand in a late Anglo-Saxon tradition including Stow and Wittering, perhaps Bosham. But the effect of this fine chancel arch wall is immeasurably enhanced by the painting (not properly revealed till the 1960s) of Christ, on an 'architectural' throne, displaying the

wounds, flanked (and approached) by apostles – the whole within grandly-conceived borders: a rather lush foliage scroll carried over the mouldings below, a 'Greek key' pattern above. Below the scroll, on either side, are the finely-realized figures of Christ giving St Peter a key and St Paul a book, backed by further architectural features (a motif of small 'stilted' arches).

Turn one's attention to the N and S nave walls, and it becomes clear that the upper-tier painted scheme is a single entity, not divided into discrete scenes as was to become normal in Romanesque art. These walls each display a processional throng – both orientated on the central figure of Christ, but with an intermediate goal: on the N side, a hexagonal image of the Heavenly City; on the S, an empty cross, held up by angels. There are trumpeting angels, noble figures of saints (haloed) and bishops (with crooks) to the N, figures crowned with the Byzantine 'kamelaukion' to the S. At its W end each wall has a sinister figure: one shows (perhaps) the fall of Antichrist, the other a devil pulling a victim by the hair down to hell. All this paintwork is in true fresco, on the lowest layer of plaster, implying a similar date to that of the building's fabric.

So what is represented? Most commentators simply class the scheme as a 'Doom', or Last Judgement. A fragment of painting on the lower tier shows the 'weighing of souls'. But it is unlike the many other early 'Dooms' (for a start, no one is actually being judged). A clue is in an early document recording the church's dedication to 'All Saints' (rather than

John the Baptist, as now), implying a different and rare scheme (even if subsuming aspects of judgement). This makes the figures on the S wall penitents, rather than the damned, as commentators have mostly assumed. We discuss early wall paintings elsewhere [above, pp. 62-69]; this is the finest, probably earliest, scheme of all.

Coombes
dedication unknown (RM-G)

Coombes Church (front cover) nestles into its hillside, accessed from a farmyard across a field, on the W side of the tidal Adur valley. On the far side the vast remains of the abandoned Beeding cement works grow ever more spectral as years go by. Coombes was one of the several prosperous villages left high-and-dry as the estuary shrank in the late Middle Ages. One enters the church through an old and beautiful S door, to be confronted at once with its notable wall paintings.

The building now protrudes from the hillside as a rectangle; earlier, it had a more normal configuration from a W tower, through the nave, to a narrower chancel. But in the 14th century the chancel was enlarged to the width of the nave. The different build can just be discerned on the exterior, but more clearly inside, where a band of painted key-pattern on the chancel arch wall stops at the former dimensions. It appears that the W tower collapsed early in the 18th century, and there are indications of this on the exterior. The W wall was of course rebuilt, but strangely

Chancel arch from nave: Christ with Sts Peter and Paul, © Roger Wilmshurst (see also p. 65)

incorporating a set of quoin-stones that appear to be long-and-short work. One small window of 11th-century character is in use, and there are signs of others; one blocked window in the S wall is distinguished by painted scroll-work in its visible splay similar to the mid-wall scroll at Clayton.

The chancel arch is plain and rather small; the abaci were at some point adorned with little carved faces at their corners. The cosy dimensions of the nave make the frescoes all the more startling, since they are experienced at eye-level or scarcely above. As true frescoes,

they are mostly in a brilliant state after careful treatment by Clive Rouse in the 1950s, the very brush-strokes discernible. It is instructive to see remains of later secco painting in various places, now almost obliterated. But there is a problem with the early paintings: brilliant as they are, they are fragmentary, interrupted not only by decayed plaster but by the insertion of later windows and monuments, and they are hard to read overall. As one enters the church, for example, one is confronted on the facing wall by a tall figure earnestly addressing an even more impressive figure (unfortunately largely obliterated by a monument) reclining on, or seated upon, a multi-arched architectural motif, amid rather grand borders. Who are they? King Herod in his palace, receiving the Magi and/or his advisors, it appears. On the opposite wall, unidentified figures in black (Jewish?) caps seem to be those who doubted the paternity of Jesus. The Visitation and Annunciation are identifiable, as also a comparatively well-preserved scene (with inscription) of the Flight into Egypt. The two walls must represent an Infancy cycle, unusual in its detail and its dramatic realization – Coombes indeed presents a whole anthology of expressive hand gestures.

The limited space of the chancel arch wall has a Christ in Majesty (almost obliterated) above, flanked by seraphim and the symbols of the four Evangelists, of which St Mark's lion is singularly well preserved. As at Clayton, Christ is shown giving a key to St Peter and a book to St Paul, but here they are a single group on the N of the arch, wonderfully placed for eye-level scrutiny. The arch itself never lost its plaster

(cf. Hardham), and preserves within, on the N side, the greatest surprise among all these vivid paintings: an 'Atlas' figure, straining with mouth agape to hold up the real or imagined building, a sort of cloud beside him, elegant pelta (double axe) patterning above.

These remarkable paintings relate to those of Clayton, though the degree of kinship cannot be simply defined (at Plumpton this is an easier problem: its surviving paintings seem a coarser version of the Clayton style and subject-matter). By comparison with Clayton's suavity and monumentality, Coombes is full of vigour – aside from the hands, limbs are often bent into an S or Z shape, their three-dimensionality indicated through rather febrile curved hatching (remote from the style of high Romanesque, as indeed Clayton is). The grand borders, of ultimately classical derivation (note the acanthus pattern), are coherent at Clayton, all over the place at Coombes. Rouse first noted that the Coombes scheme was by a different hand; there would seem to be a generational difference, too, with a new set of masters in probably the late 11th century using and adapting the old pattern-books.

Greatham – *see Hardham*

Hardham, St Botolph (RM-G)

Hardham church – dedicated to the Saxon Saint Botolph but, according to an early-medieval document, to St George – is famous

Chancel W wall, Eve milking with Adam pruning above, © David Boys

Chancel W wall, Adam and Eve, © David Boys (see also p. 66)

for its astonishingly complete cycle of wall paintings: c.40 scenes survive, though some are very faded, despite (or in part because of) many restoration attempts since they were rediscovered in 1866. They are in true fresco on the lowest layer of plaster, which indicates they are contemporary with the rubble fabric of the walls. These walls, whitewashed externally, are largely of local Pulborough stone, with numerous Roman brick fragments. Though now an inconspicuous village, Hardham is a location of ancient significance: close to a Roman station on Stane Street, overlooking the floodplain of the navigable River Arun at the point where it is crossed by a causeway marking the start of another Roman road, the E–W 'Greensand Way'. To the S are fine ruins of a medieval priory. Such a location

on ancient highways is characteristic of some other interesting early churches (Buncton, Clayton, Old Shoreham, Sompting).

The simple building has not been much changed. Its proportions, its quoin stones and the plain, quite broad chancel arch seem to be early post-Conquest indicators. The blocked S doorway with its massive lintel is original. Two later Gothic windows were inserted in the chancel, as was a squint to the S for an anchorite (who was funded by the subsequent St Richard of Chichester).

The wall paintings are in two tiers. On the nave E, N and S walls there is a detailed Nativity/Infancy cycle above (at one point, with remarkable wind-blown curtains). Below, the most discussed part is the cycle to the NW, probably representing the Life (and particularly the martyrdom) of St George. In one scene the saint, on horseback, slays an enemy. At the historic Battle of Antioch (1098) St George miraculously appeared with two other warrior-saints to rescue the beleaguered crusaders. Of course St George was already revered in a warrior role; nevertheless no earlier representations of him are known in England, and maybe 1098 is a *terminus post quem* for the painting, though we cannot be certain. Facing these scenes on the S wall is the tale of Dives and the beggar Lazarus.

The chancel-arch wall carries remarkable painting. Above the arch, in place of Christ, is the Lamb of God. The Annunciation is marked by a Latin inscription in Lombardic lettering. Angels on either side are vividly delineated, with agitated garments and the Anglo-Saxon 'anguished stoop' reminiscent of 'Winchester School' art of c.1000. The main haloes are picked out in a copper-derived bluish green. Alas, the 'Labours of the Months' only partially survive, since at some point in the 19th century the plaster on the arch was hacked off to reveal the stonework.

The far (E) side of the same wall has the most astonishing of the Hardham paintings – telling the story of Adam and Eve (with apocryphal elements), shown as if on a tapestry – see the painted hooks. The gesticulating, elongated naked figures are often justly termed expressionistic; but note too such details as the rather elegant serpent, the water in which the repentant pair half-submerge themselves (its apparently 'blue' waves derived from white with a carbon-black admixture), and Adam amid the branches of a tree, evidently pruning it, while Eve milks a cow.

Paintings on the other chancel walls are hard to discern, but show grand subjects: Passion and Resurrection scenes; the Elders of the Apocalypse, seraphim, doubtless a Christ in Majesty before a new E window was put in. The nave W wall is almost indecipherable, but seems to have displayed scenes of Hell and the Damned (Dives among them).

Stylistically, the Hardham paintings are puzzling. No-one doubts they are all of similar date, but at least two very different hands are seen: many of the figures are astonishingly perfunctory (or, in their patterning, 'folksy'); elsewhere the hand of a self-assured, expressive master (or masters), though in an older, Anglo-Saxon tradition, can be discerned. Very little relates anything here to the manner of Clayton, Plumpton or Coombes, with the sole exception of the 'architectural' motif of little arches, here used to divide discrete elements of the narratives. The grand borders of Clayton and Coombes are absent, though there is some fictive drapery beneath the lower scenes. For over a century it has been commonplace to 'pair' Hardham with Clayton, but this is clearly untenable.

It may be too speculative, but it could be that the iconography is orientated towards the experience of a largely rural congregation, emphasized by the prominent position of the Labours of the Month and Lamb of God, as well the rustic elements of the Adam and Eve cycle; while the minatory Dives and Lazarus cycle is an exaltation of the poor and humble over the wealthy. The very completeness of Hardham gives us an unrivalled chance to assess the layout of the frescoes for ourselves.

*

Only a mile or so S of Hardham, but on the other bank of the Arun, in a tiny unspoilt settlement away from roads, stands **GREATHAM** church – remarkable even among Downland churches for its untouched simplicity. Its materials are like those of Hardham (with Pulborough stone quoins), and its date is probably similar. There is no division between nave and chancel. Whether any wall painting survives under the internal whitewash is unknown. The blocked N door is curiously narrow, the S porch has a slab – probably a former altar table – of Sussex 'marble' on its floor. One datable feature is a small blocked window of 11th-century character, its stonework visible only from the outside, in the E wall (see pp. 6, 23, 33 & 42). Not far away at **WIGGONHOLT** is another single-celled church.

General view from NE as drawn by Petrie in 1804, showing the Downs in the background and the turret on the N transept; the E window, apparently with timber glazing bars, was later replaced (© Sussex Archaeological Society, Sharpe Collection no.310) (see also p. 50)

North Stoke, St Mary
[Churches Conservation Trust]

The church consists of nave, chancel and N and S transepts, but it is not a conventional planned cruciform church. The earliest part of the building is the nave (remains of narrow round-headed windows close to the transept W walls, 11th-century), which is wider than the 13th-century chancel, with no provision for a crossing tower between. The transepts were simply added on to the nave in the late 13th or 14th century. At about the same time the chancel arch was inserted, and the wall flanking it fitted out with recesses, which served as image niches for the reredoses of subsidiary altars at the E end of the nave; this is a rare survival of evidence for the placing of altars on either side of the chancel arch. Further evidence for the liturgical use of the church before the Reformation exists in the S transept, which was used as a side chapel. The sill of the E window is dropped to form another altar reredos recess, and there is a piscina in the S wall, close to the SE corner. There is similar evidence in the N transept, so by the early 14th century there were four subsidiary altars in a line across the church. Additionally, in the S transept W wall is a seating recess of two bays with two arch heads resting on a reused earlier corbel.

The service of the high altar in the chancel is shown not only by the existence of yet another piscina in the S wall but by the adjacent sedilia of three seat recesses for the clergy officiating at the Mass. These seats are 'graded', that is they rise in level to accommodate the steps in the floor from the main level to the raised sanctuary where the altar stood beneath the E window. On either side of the window are image brackets supported on corbels with 13th-century leaf carving.

The church has a representative selection of Gothic window styles. In the chancel side walls are lancets with plain pointed heads; the transept end walls have two-light 'geometrical' windows with foiled circles at the top; and the transept E walls have three-light windows with intersecting tracery, including some cusping. The triple lancet in the chancel E wall is modern, but the Petrie watercolour of 1804 shows a large round-headed window with what appear to be wooden mullions and transom.

An unusual feature is the timber bell-turret, which protrudes through the slope of the N transept roof. The roof timbers, visible in the S transept and nave, appear to be medieval. There are precious survivals of 14th-century coloured glass: a detached panel in the chancel showing the Coronation of the Virgin, and fragments of another in the S transept E window.

Other interesting medieval features include the carving of the fingers of a little hand, apparently holding up the N side of the chancel arch; a strange carved ?ram's head in the S transept; a bulbous lead-lined font of c.1200; considerable remains (though hard to make out) of painted foliage and fruit designs on the chancel-arch wall and niches; three early gravestones in the graveyard. In its fine, secluded location, this is a most rewarding church to visit.

*

Only half a mile S by path and bridge (but with no direct road) is **SOUTH STOKE**, with a quaint church of early origin, much restored; another mile S (again, no road) is **BURPHAM**, with a large Romanesque and later church beside the massive ramparts of a deserted Saxon *burh* (fortified town).

Old Shoreham, St Nicholas

Historically the position of the church is important: close to the River Adur, it is near to the crossing point of an ancient routeway running E–W along the southern edge of the Downs. The old toll bridge, which replaced an earlier ferry, survives. Farther W, another important early church stands to the N of this route (Sompting: see below).

Tie beam with billet moulding (see also p. 40)

St Nicolas's is a complex building which developed out of an Anglo-Saxon church, represented by the present nave. On the N side, the wall steps back close to the W end, which suggests that there was a tower or some sort of western annex here. In this part of the wall is a tall blocked opening, with typical Anglo-Saxon proportions. There must have been a chancel to the E of this nave, presumably under the present tower, which may have been built on its footprint in the 12th century. At this point the church was given a cruciform layout, with transepts on either side of the tower forming the arms of the cross and a new eastern compartment forming the upper limb. This may have taken the form of an extended apse, and there were probably apses flanking it to the E of the transepts, judging by the remains of features in their E walls, which are thought to have been arches leading into the apses. At the same time the nave was remodelled with opposed N and S doorways, both now blocked.

The crossing tower has double belfry openings flanked by blind arches and with circular lights above (compare East Meon (H), where the belfry lights are single, however, and flanked by open arches). Internally it has four richly decorated arches of several orders. The carved decoration is restricted to the sides of the arches visible to people standing in the nave or facing E in the crossing space itself. They serve to draw attention to that space, which may mean that the main altar was in this central position (there were probably others in the apses). Of the various decorative motifs in the stonework – which include a very feline-looking face mask at the crown of the western arch – the pattern of the hood mould over the eastern arch is unusual. It consists of a series of small rosettes linked by a relief band, and has been described as a 'daisy chain'. Though different in detail, this is similar to the hood moulds of the arcade arches at Steyning, suggesting that the same expert craftsmen were at work on both churches around 1140.

Later in the Middle Ages the apses were removed or rebuilt; the central one became a conventional chancel around 1300, and on the N side a larger chapel developed. This has since been removed, but evidence for it remains in the shape of a piscina in the N wall of the chancel. This means that there must have been an altar to the N of it; altars have to be in a covered space, hence there must have been a chapel here.

There are rare items of woodwork in the church. The most obvious is the screen across the arch into the chancel, with trefoil-

Central tower, chancel and S transept from SE

headed narrow lights of about 1300, but much restored; the survival of woodwork of this date is rare. Even rarer the high beam across the nave above the arch into the tower; this has billet ornament of 12th-century type, though a much later date has been proposed in the *Victoria County History*. In the chancel another beam carved with 13th-century dogtooth ornament; the background is painted bright red, but it is not clear whether this is original.

Parham, St Peter

The church stands in the park close to the house; there are no obvious traces of the village which was here until the late 1770s. St Peter's is a simple building: nave and chancel, with a W tower and SE chapel, the latter added around 1545 by the then lord of the manor. His successor in the early 19th century is said to have rebuilt the tower – possibly just the belfry stage – and added the N transept in a campaign that lasted until about 1820. In the

N wall of the nave are indications of a blocked arcade, maybe of 12th-century date, implying the existence of a N aisle. This may have been removed at the time the transept was built.

The interior of the church was totally reordered with furnishings typical of the 'auditory churches' of the 17th and 18th centuries, of which Parham is a very late example. There is a two-decker pulpit with sounding board, and the nave is filled with box pews; between the nave and chancel is a screen with wide lights and frilly cusping of Gothick design. The original chancel arch has been replaced by a broad elliptical opening. The nave ceiling is plastered and coved, with a Classical cornice. The N transept was intended as the squire's 'pew' and has a domestic fireplace in its N wall.

In the chancel there is panelling matching the nave pews, which includes a reredos in the embrasure of the E window, and a communion rail with turned spindles. The 'modernisation' did not however include the insertion of a

General view from S

Interior facing E with post-Reformation furniture (see also p. 56)

Venetian E window. The chancel ceiling with tracery ribwork was added *c.*1850.

An unusual survival from the medieval period is the lead font. Stylistically it is dated to the 14th century, a late date for the use of this material: most lead fonts are Romanesque. Its decoration is also unusual, consisting only of the repeated text ✠*IHC NAZAR* and heraldic shields bearing the arms of Andrew Peverell, the probable donor, who was Knight of the Shire in the parliament of 1351.

Petworth, Sacred Heart
(Roman Catholic)

This church was designed by F A Walters (1849–1931), a prolific architect for the Roman Catholic Church, whose work includes the sacristy at Downside Abbey. Locally his church building is represented by the interesting Holy Ghost at the Franciscan friary at Chilworth (Blackheath), Surrey, 20 miles

General view from SE (see also p. 20)

north of Petworth, and – closer to SDNP – by Winchester St Peter, Grayshott St Joseph (the latter only two miles north of the Park boundary), and part of Brighton, St Joseph. Later, his firm built St Pancras in Lewes (see below).

Sacred Heart is built in a revived Decorated style, and has a clerestoried nave and side

Interior facing NE

aisles and a prominent south-west porch. It has transepts, but no crossing tower; instead, there is an octagonal turret in the armpit between the south transept and the apse at the east end, surmounted by a slender copper flèche. The windows have elaborate tracery. Internally the apse is vaulted, but the nave has an open timber roof. The nave arcades have continuous mouldings, with capitals only on the inner order.

Petworth, St Mary the Virgin

The view of the church tower up Lombard Street is strikingly unusual, with its gaunt brick upper part and low pyramidal capping. It has had a chequered career. When drawn by S H Grimm in 1789 it had a tall spire covered in shingles. In 1804 this was taken down and replaced by a parapet with corner pinnacles, but a new stone spire was built to the design of Charles – later Sir Charles – Barry, the architect of the Houses of Parliament. Barry's spire became a familiar townscape feature, appearing in early photographs, in Turner's views of Petworth house and park, and in numerous picture postcards, until in 1947 it was declared unsafe and demolished; the top of the tower was later rebuilt as it is today.

Barry's restoration in 1827–29 also included the addition of the S aisle, connected to the body of the church by an arcade of elegant arches built of fine Portland stone, which contrasts with the rest of the fabric, which is in local sandstone. The N aisle and its arcade are 14th-century, though Barry rebuilt the piers; they were remodelled again in the 1903 restoration. At that time the unusual coffered ceiling over the nave was inserted. The remainder of the church is medieval: the chancel 13th-century, the chapel of St Thomas of Canterbury to the N of the chancel somewhat later and the N transept earlier. The N transept has an upper floor, which was the private pew of the owners of Petworth House, though now disused. On the outside of the church can be seen the steps and a blocked doorway which afforded direct access from the house to the upper floor. This had evidently been a chapel in medieval times, since there is a piscina in the SE corner; in the W wall are the remains of a window, probably of Norman date, and the earliest architectural feature in the building.

Tower from SE, medieval masonry below, modern brick above

Petworth, former chapel, W elevation

Interior facing NW showing W gallery and (extreme right) part of private gallery chapel for Petworth House (see also p. 74)

The influence of the successive families at the 'big house', who were patrons of the living and financed the major restoration**s,** is in evidence throughout the church. It includes a memorial tablet in the tower to the Percy family, the original owners of Petworth House, and the imposing life-size seated figure of the 3rd Earl of Egremont, who paid for Barry's work, in the N aisle. There is a monument to another notable local family in St Thomas's chapel. It commemorates Sir John Dawtrey (†1542) and his wife, and its form continues the tradition of the late-medieval Easter Sepulchre: a heavily framed recess above a tomb chest,

with small kneeling figures taking the place of brasses or mural painting. The repainting of the monument is modern, but it gives an impression of its original 16th-century finish.

Much of the glass in the windows dates from the 1903 restoration, which was carried out by Kempe and Tower. C E Kempe is noted for his coloured glass work (in the 'greenery-yallery' tradition), which is ubiquitous in Sussex, where he was based. One window in St Mary's stands out, however: the rose window over the chancel arch, which was inserted by Barry in the late 1820s. The glass here is German of about 1840, and its strong colours contrast strongly with Kempe's more delicate shades.

To the SE of the church, a little way down East Street, the former **Unitarian chapel**, dated 1819, since used as a school and currently a private house; a pedimented building with large round-headed windows.

*

At nearby **TILLINGTON** the tower with an unusual 'Scots Crown' spire was added in 1807; its position at the E end of the S aisle is also unusual. There are 15th-century examples of this rare form of capping at Newcastle Cathedral and St Giles's Cathedral, Edinburgh (hence its name).

Poynings, Holy Trinity (RM-G)

The church is splendidly located at the foot of Devil's Dyke, within a fold of the Downs and on a small hill. It is an impressive building, cruciform with a central tower, and is exceptional among Downland churches: effectively of a single period – Decorated to early Perpendicular, uncommon in this area – and rather closely dateable, since it was built to replace an earlier, Domesday Book, church under the wills of Michael and his wife Joan de Poynings at the end of the 1360s. It has been suggested that some of the earlier church's fabric survives in the S transept, but this is not apparent. There is a strip of early glazed tiles, however, in front of the altar. Within the

SDNP only Alfriston, in the Cuckmere valley (ESx), is of similar date and form, though with a spire.

The porch to the N has been reconstructed, but not detrimentally (it contained the grave of Michael's grandson). The church interior is noble, unspoiled and rather austere, with a long, high chancel and spacious transepts, once treated as separate chapels (the S one contained Michael's grave; it is accessed through a 14th-century wooden screen). High in the E window of the N transept is an elegant painted-glass scene of the Annunciation. Nearly all the window tracery is in keeping with the period of construction, though the 17th-century S window of the S transept was brought from Chichester Cathedral in 1843, when repairs were carried out. (Incidentally the **Zion Chapel**, in the village street by the pub, proclaims the same date on its sober, pedimented façade: did a team of builders simply move from an Anglican

Exterior from S, showing crossing tower, S transept and part of nave (further illustrations on pp. 55, 59 & 77)

View into SE corner of chancel, showing liturgical furnishing and box pew

to a Nonconformist commission?) There are unusually early (17th-century) box pews facing each other in the chancel; there is a characteristically vernacular Jacobean pulpit; remains of several monumental brasses are in the S transept, as are some 14th-century glazed tiles and a tie beam of 1625. The well-preserved sedilia, piscina and font accord beautifully with the whole ensemble. One mystery remains. A quite large patch of the nave S wall has been cleared of whitewash to reveal post-Reformation texts; but these appear to overlie faint remains of medieval wall painting. Might more have survived elsewhere?

*

A couple of miles W of Poynings is **EDBURTON**, in an equally fine location under the Downs, with a W tower and also with a noble interior – most of it slightly earlier, but with similar Decorated tracery. Its unusual feature is a small lead font with delicate low-relief scrollwork. And a couple of miles E is **PYECOMBE** – basically Norman, with another, larger, lead font, similarly adorned.

Singleton, St Mary
(formerly St John the Evangelist)

Singleton is the main centre of settlement in the Hundred to which it gives its name. Its landed endowment recorded in the Domesday survey implies a 'superior' church, and a major Anglo-Saxon minster would be expected. But only the W tower appears to be of early and possibly pre-Conquest date, and the remainder of the building has none of the hallmarks of a post-Conquest successor to a minster.

The interpretation of the tower is not straightforward. Seen from the W end of the N aisle, its NE quoin continues down to ground level, usually a sign of a free-standing structure. This suggests a lordly tower-church, like those at Jevington and East Dean (ESx; see below), rather than a regional minster.

However, excavations in the 1970s discovered evidence for an earlier nave, but this has never been properly published; if that is correct, it is not clear why the E wall of the added tower was not built off the end wall of the nave (the usual procedure) rather than being a separate entity with its own eastern quoins.

The tower is rather daunting with its sheer walls covered by uninteresting-looking rendering, but has features of importance for its late Anglo-Saxon dating. In each of the external walls there is a window at ground-floor level with double splays (i.e. they widen towards the outside aperture as well as to the inside). In the N and S walls they are off-centre, probably because there were originally doorways to the W of them, but this cannot be proved because of the rendering and the massive buttress against the S wall; such doorways would be entirely appropriate for a tower-nave church. Inside the church there is a gable-headed doorway high up in the W wall of the nave, another typical late Anglo-Saxon feature. This indicates that there must have been a structure to the E of the tower, with the door giving access to its roof space. The tower arch, leading into it at ground floor level, does not have its original arch head, but the jambs are built of through-stones, also an Anglo-Saxon characteristic.

The body of the church is a standard aisled nave and chancel. The chancel is 13th-century, but there is debate about the nave arcades; it has been suggested that they are also 13th-century but remodelled in the 15th. The published plan of the church shows them

Interior facing W (further illustrations on pp. 53 & 54)

and the aisle walls as 15th: the junction of the N arcade, the E wall of the N aisle and the chancel N wall is thickened up to take the rood loft stair, which is likely to be later rather than earlier. The doorways at both levels survive. In the angle between the porch W wall and the nave there is evidence for another stairway, meaning that there was originally an upper storey to the porch. The main windows are

General view from SE

of two lights in the aisles, 15th-century, and of three lights in the chancel, probably 16th, all with simple tracery and slightly depressed pointed heads.

The timber W gallery is thought to date from the 17th century.

Sompting, St Mary

Away from the modern village and standing on the southern slope of the Downs, the church is a dominant feature of the landscape and a distraction to drivers on the A27 trunk road below it. A local road runs northward past the E end of the church, crossing the entire breadth of the Downs at this point, leading eventually to Steyning, on the northern fringe of SDNP.

The instantly recognisable feature of the St Mary's is the 'Rhenish helm' at the top of the W tower. The name for this type of capping

is a reference to the many examples to be found in the Rhineland and adjacent areas; its occurrence at Sompting is unique amongst English medieval churches, though there is a Victorian example at Hawkley (H), about halfway between Petersfield and Selborne, also in SDNP.

The Sompting helm was long considered to be an Anglo-Saxon structure, but the upper part of the tower is now recognised as a Romanesque addition to a pre-Conquest lower storey, previously the western part of the aisle-less nave. It has further been discovered by tree-ring analysis that many of the timbers of the helm are of early 14th-century date. There is still considerable debate about the structural development of the tower and its cap, and the dates of their constituent parts.

The long, narrow nave survives from the late Anglo-Saxon period, when it would have been longer: internally the W wall was added when the superstructure of the tower was built over the end bay of the nave, probably at the end of the 11th century. Between the nave and what is now the base of the tower is an off-centre arch; its eccentric position is usually explained by postulating an altar against the tower side of the wall to the N of the archway. The E end of the original church is now not known because of later rebuilding; the date of the chancel is unclear.

In 1184 the Templars acquired the church and added a N transept with two chapels to the E, entered by arches with plain pointed heads, circular piers and multi-scalloped capitals,

Tower and part of nave from SW (see also p. 40)

typical of the period. The chapels have high-quality rib vaults. The Templars also built a structure on the S side, converted into a transept in modern times, though its floor level is considerably lower. A shallow eastern projection is rib-vaulted and has waterleaf capitals. In 1306 the Templars were replaced by the Knights Hospitaller, who built a chapel on the N side of the nave at the W end; this became ruinous, but was replaced in 1971 by

Romanesque Christ in Majesty panel

Two-bay E chapel of N transept

a parish room. In the S wall of this room is the piscina which served the original chapel.

The church contains numerous examples of early-medieval carved stonework, including the capitals of the arch between the nave and the tower. Other fragments have been reused in later contexts, for example two pieces of late 11th-century acanthus frieze forming the head of a piscina in the chancel. There is a panel with a charming portrait of a cleric with a crozier at a reading (?writing) desk, and, displayed on an arm projecting from the N wall of the nave, a group of three stones cemented together: on the W face two of them bear elements of an arched frieze, while on the E side the group has been treated as a single panel and re-cut with a portrayal of Christ in Majesty (early 13th-century).

Steyning, Sts Andrew and Cuthman

A lot of research has been devoted to this church in recent years, but many questions remain unanswered. Its history goes back to the early Anglo-Saxon period, when Cuthman is claimed to have founded the church; Steyning is one of only two Sussex churches with a saint's legend (Bishopstone (ESx) is the other). It also has royal connections, being mentioned in the will of King Alfred, whose father was originally buried here. Two churches are recorded here in Domesday Book (1086), but no early fabric survives, apart from two grave covers, which are on display in the porch. One of these belongs to a type known elsewhere in WSx at Chithurst and Stedham.

Part of the present church is the remnant of a large and very elaborate building of 12th-century date. The arch from the S aisle to the transept, with its carved capitals and shaft ring suggest a date shortly after 1100 for the original E end of the church, most of which was demolished in the Elizabethan period. The magnificent nave and side aisles (exceptionally they are not add-ons here) were built on later in the century. The present 'chancel' arch was the western arch of a large crossing tower and is richly carved with Romanesque decoration, as are the arcade arches of the nave and the clerestory windows above. Where these join the W wall of the nave there are signs that the arcades once continued farther to the W – at least one bay, and possibly two. This end of the church was altered shortly after 1600, however, when the present W tower was built;

N arcade looking NW (further illustrations on pp. 13, 30, 39, 40 & 69)

it replaced the crossing tower, which had been demolished with the E end of the building.

Inside the porch (built in the 15th century, modified in 1766 – see date stone) is the original 12th-century doorway, and the wooden door leaf and its ironwork may be original too. To the E of the porch a broad flat Romanesque buttress with nook shafts. It is built of ashlar, like so much of the 12th-century fabric, but unlike the surrounding aisle wall. This may have been rebuilt as later windows were inserted, but it is noticeable that the N aisle wall is also of flint rubble, while containing the only surviving Norman-period window. Below that window is a short stretch of decorated hood mould belonging to the Romanesque N doorway, which was replaced by one with a pointed arch in the 13th or 14th century, subsequently blocked in brick. Yet another fabric is represented in the tower walling: diaper work consisting of ashlar blocks alternating with squares of knapped flint.

Notable fittings inside the church include the oak panels dated 1522 below the E window, brought in from elsewhere; Royal Arms high up on the nave W wall, Queen Anne, 1703; and the St Cuthman window near the S door, by Christopher Whall, *c.*1921; the porch window of 1939, possibly by his daughter Veronica. Earlier windows by Whall can be seen in the side aisles of **St Luke, MILLAND (WSx)**.

*

Jarvis Hall, on Jarvis Lane, is the former **Trinity Chapel**, which had originated in 1835 as the place of worship of the Countess of

General view from SE

Huntingdon's Connexion; Wesleyan from 1841 to 1878, it was subsequently used by the Salvation Army and the Plymouth Brethren interspersed by secular uses. It was converted into flats in 1987. The building is neo-Classical in style, with tall pilasters surmounted by a giant pediment; two large round-headed windows and two oculi; a square-framed doorway with fanlight.

At the N end of the High Street the road bends sharply and becomes Horsham Road (*en route* to **Buncton**, see above). Here the so-called Penn's House, of 17th-century or earlier date, was converted in 1678 to a **Quaker Meeting House**. It is a timber-framed building in the domestic tradition, now clad in rubblestone, brick and tile-hanging.

Stopham, St Mary's church

St Mary's is one of those churches that the experts argue about: is it Anglo-Saxon or Romanesque (Norman)? Its apparently nave-and-chancel structure is common to both styles, but looking down the church inside gives the impression that the chancel was originally a square space between the nave and another element to the E. The published plan suggests that the extra space between that square and the E window may be the remnant of an earlier apse, later squared off. If so, the additional masonry was fitted very neatly to the existing walling, because there are no obvious joints in the N and S chancel walls. If an apse did exist, then the plan consisted of three elements: nave, chancel and apse, which is a typical layout for a post-Conquest church (compare Newhaven, ESx, where the square chancel carries a tower, and Easton, Hants; the latter in SDNP, see above). Strong arguments have been put forward, however, for an Anglo-Saxon date for the details of the S door surround; the door on the opposite side, which similarly has a very tall internal arch, has different capitals, which can only be seen from the modern vestry. They are of the 'cushion' type, common in English Romanesque

General view from SE

architecture (though not in Normandy), and they may have been introduced before the Conquest. Widely splayed round-headed windows in the chancel side walls, probably late 12th-century; that on the N cuts an earlier window whose head, made of a single stone, and part of whose E jamb can still be seen externally, while part of the jamb is preserved inside near the NE corner of the chancel.

N of the chancel arch there is a shallow recess with a pointed arch, presumably inserted in the 13th century or later to serve as the reredos for a subsidiary altar set below it. The altar will have been removed in the late 1540s as part of the Protestant reordering.

Interior facing E; note altar reredos recess N of chancel arch (see also pp. 47 & 71))

The W tower seems to have been rebuilt about 1600. The window in the W wall is of the 'reduced' medieval type common after the Reformation, and the blocked W door has a low head derived from the so-called Tudor arch.

An outstanding feature of the interior is a series of brasses to the Barttelot family, set in the floor of the nave and chancel and protected by carpet. The Barttelots have been associated with Stopham, probably since the Norman Conquest, and became lords of the manor by the 16th century. The earliest brasses date from the 15th. Most are set in slabs of Sussex 'marble'. There are wall monuments to the family throughout the church. Set in the Perpendicular-style E window is heraldic glass of 1638 recording the Barttelots and the families with which they intermarried. In the N window of the nave glass by a Flemish glazier of around 1600 commemorates a Barttelot ancestor, Brian de Stopham, who died in 1273.

Stoughton, St Mary

St Mary's is almost certainly the high-status church recorded here in 1086. It has many of the characteristics of a Saxo-Norman building: tall thin walls with much pitched and some counterpitched ('herringbone') masonry, double-splayed windows and *porticus*, or transept-like chapels flanking the nave; there are no side aisles. The most imposing feature is the chancel arch with triple shafts and roll mouldings, like Bosham, a feature that also appears in simplified form at Clayton and

elsewhere. The arches into the *porticus*, however, were replaced around 1200.

There were few additions to the basic structure. No added side aisles: presumably the *porticus*-transepts offered sufficient space to contain the additional altars that became *de rigueur* around the time the arches into them were rebuilt, and presumably enlarged. The S transept was heightened in the 14th century to form a low tower; the change in fabric about two-thirds of the way up can clearly be seen from the W. In the 17th century an attractive brick porch was added on the S side.

An odd feature in the appearance of the church is the number of stones apparently missing from the W exterior wall of the nave. These are very regularly distributed and represent the holes running right through the wall to take the horizontal poles of the original builders' scaffolding; they are known

General view from SW, showing put-log holes in W wall, the S porch and the change of fabric in the tower (see also p. 36)

E end of nave, chancel arch in centre and arch into N *porticus* left

as 'put-log holes'. They have a flat stone 'lid' which kept the pressure off the horizontal pole. When the scaffolding was taken down, these holes will have been blocked up with spare fragments of stone or flint set in mortar, a rather loose fill, kept in place (and out of sight) by the rendering on the wall. Once this decayed, frost and rain, not to mention nesting birds, would soon loosen the outer part of the fill, leaving the shallow voids that can be seen today.

West Chiltington, St Mary (RM-G)

Hardham and West Chiltington churches, only some three miles apart, are distinguished by two of the most extensive sets of medieval wall paintings to survive not only in the Downs, but in the whole country. Yet they are remarkably different. At Hardham an apparently unified

scheme, which may be as early as the 11th century, covers nearly all the interior of the small building. St Mary's, W. Chiltington, has no known painting that predates the later 12th century, but in contrast retains cycles or fragments probably from every subsequent century till the Reformation (indeed later: there is a 17th-century painted text high on the W wall); it is almost an anthology of the art-form.

S aisle, painting of angel, © Lisa Fisher (see also p. 64)

The village is in the undulating Lower Greensand countryside E of Pulborough, and the church is beautifully located on a slight mound, closing the view down its oldest street. The building stone comes largely from the Hythe Beds of the Greensand; the roof is of 'Horsham slabs'. 'Like a French village church' (to quote Ian Nairn), it has a large but stumpy central tower with spire (dating in its present form from 1602). The main fabric of the building is early Romanesque in character, though there may be earlier, Anglo-Saxon, material incorporated, and there are various later additions and modifications. In particular a S aisle, roofed continuously with the nave, was added in the late 12th century – it has a round-headed Romanesque W window, but the arches punched through to the nave, and another to the E, are pointed, and clearly 'transitional'. A chantry chapel was added to the E end of the aisle in the 14th century, so chantry and aisle are parallel with the original chancel and nave. An astonishingly long hagioscope (squint) gives a view of the chancel from the aisle E end.

One enters through a fine N porch reconstructed from ancient timbers and stonework. Ahead are the thick pillars, with rough acanthus-derived capitals, separating nave from aisle; the arcade carries simple decorative painting, but on the wall above it is a dramatic narrative cycle, representing the Passion and (on spandrel below, opposite the door) the Resurrection. Turn round, and on the nave N wall the equally fine companion cycle of the Nativity is seen. Both are of 13th-century character, and are evidently intended to match and complement each other, yet do not seem to be of quite the same date: the Nativity came first, and has a lingering touch of Romanesque formality; the Passion, full of agitated movement, with a more brilliant colour range, is thoroughly Gothic in manner. Presumably an intended scheme was halted, no doubt through lack of funds, then resumed a few years later. Individual scenes on each wall are framed in painted trefoil arches (more solid-looking on the N wall, with dignified angels in some of the spandrels).

These two beautiful cycles are neither the oldest, nor the most unusual painted schemes in the church. The E end of the aisle carries damaged, but remarkable work from the 12th century, probably in true fresco: apostles or prophets, as well as fictive wall-hangings, within the arch, and on its face censing or trumpeting angels, notable for the Byzantinesque 'damp-fold' modelling of the garments. High above this arch, by a walkway to the rood-loft, is a much later (mid 14th-century) but even rarer painting: a 'Solomonic' (endless) knot in red ochre, enclosed in a sort of belt surmounted by a fleur-de-lys. The endless knot, a kind of guilloche, is an ancient motif found in many cultures (particularly in Roman mosaics), but what is it doing here? Does it relate to Edward III's claim to the French throne and institution of the Order of the Garter – if so, why? Or is it really a 'demon-trap'?

There are several other paintings. Decorative work varies from the remarkably crude (on the nave arcade) to refined masonry and foliage patterning on the chancel arch wall. In the 14th century a window was inserted into the nave N wall (interrupting the Nativity cycle): on its splay is a good example of that strange late-medieval image, the 'Sunday Christ' or 'Warning to Sabbath-Breakers' – a Christ-figure wounded by the tools of those who work on the Sabbath. W of the same window is the large but now almost invisible figure of St Christopher, protector of travellers. Finally, from the last period of medieval art (15th–16th centuries), the single small, delightful figure of an angel playing a fiddle, with a fragment of text, has been removed from a position high above the chancel arch, where it could scarcely be seen, to the N side of the arch itself; apparently it formed part of a Last Judgement. The arch itself must have been raised, and the floor of the nave lowered, to assist the view from 17th-century galleries at the W, now removed. This well-kept church, with its eventful building history and unmatched paintings, is one of the most rewarding of the whole area.

Woolbeding, All Hallows

It stands close to Woolbeding House: only the churchyard wall separates All Hallows' from the hall grounds. This proximity to the local 'big house' is a common feature of rural churches, shared with several others in the area of the National Park. There was a church here at the time of Domesday Book (1086), but the only part of the early church to survive is the nave. The nave N and S walls are embellished with typical late Anglo-Saxon pilaster strips, as

General view from SE

seen at Corhampton (H; see above), and the proportions of the nave are similar, though not identical, to those of Corhampton. There the similarities end: the blocked S door here is shorter than the N door at Corhampton, and lacks the surrounding stripwork; it is possibly a later insertion, but since the wall is covered with roughcast it is not possible to see whether there is any evidence for this. The original quoins are visible on the N side of the church, and they are not of the long-and-short type seen at Corhampton, but rather 'side alternate', that is to say a series of flat stones laid with their sides visible alternately in the N and the E or W walls respectively; there are no 'long' stones set vertically.

The original chancel may have survived until 1728, when it was repaired or rebuilt, but the present chancel is a new build of 1870; the chancel arch has been replaced at least twice, and its original form cannot even be conjectured. In 1728 also the W tower was built by Sir Richard Mill, lord of the manor, at a cost of £74 2s.; it replaced an earlier 'stipple', which may have been a timber belfry. There is a date stone in the lower part of the present tower, but it has been suggested that it might have been moved from the chancel in 1870, when the porch to the S of the tower was also added.

In the N window of the chancel and the SW window of the nave is 16th-century continental glass, which had been brought from Mottisfont Priory (H) and used to glaze the E window of the 18th-century chancel. There are angels and human figures, probably parts of the biblical scenes of the Annunciation and the Passion. Another apparent survival from the 1728 chancel is the wooden reredos panel, now mounted on the S wall of the chancel, bearing the Creed, Lord's Prayer and the Commandments. Probably of the same date is the communion rail with slender mahogany balusters.

Alfriston, St Andrew

St Andrew's stands on a mound close to the Cuckmere river, and is unusual on several counts. Like Poynings (WSx), it is an aisle-less cruciform church with central tower, a form usually associated with the Romanesque, but the date here is probably 1340–1400; it appears to have been built in one go, with few later interventions until the 19th century, so like the later Glynde (ESx) it is a rare one-period church. Unlike either of the two comparanda, however, there is no evidence for an earlier church, and in this part of ESx there is no Domesday record to fall back on.

St Christopher window (further illustrations on pp. 50 & 52)

General view from NW

The church is built of knapped flints with sandstone dressings; it is symmetrical, and the nave and chancel are of equal length. The doors and windows are fairly regularly disposed, including matching ogee-headed lowside windows in the chancel N and S walls, an unusual feature. Stylistically it represents the transition from the Decorated style to the Perpendicular; there are two-light windows in the earlier style, and larger ones with panel tracery typical of Perp endicular, while the nave W window combines features of both styles. Below that is a doorway with a square hood and decorated spandrels, presumably the processional entrance to the church, since there were opposed doorways in the side walls for everyday use, the one on the N now blocked.

There is good evidence of medieval liturgical practice. In the S wall of the chancel is a piscina and three-bay sedilia with level seats (like Poynings, but unlike North Stoke, WSx), and piscinas in the E wall of the transepts indicate that there were altars there, too, as at North Stoke. In the N wall of the chancel is an Easter Sepulchre under an ogee arch, where the consecrated Host was placed on Good Friday and removed on the morning of Easter Day, symbolising the burial and Resurrection of Christ. The figures are from a 19th-century reredos removed in 1987. Also in the chancel, the tie-beam of the roof retains hooks and staples used to hang a veil over the sanctuary during Lent.

Other medieval survivals are the timbers of the crown-post roofs (except over the S transept), some fragments of 14th-century glass in the N transept N window, showing two saints, one of them possibly St Alphege, and a painted consecration cross N of the altar. The choir stalls and communion rail are of around 1905.

*

South of the church stands the **Clergy House** [National Trust], another rare survival. It is a timber-framed hall house of Wealden type. Off the NW corner of the Tye, the open green area, is the former **Congregational Chapel** of 1801 (see p. 18), a plain four-square building with two tiers of windows, and inside a timber gallery on three sides supported on Tuscan columns.

Berwick, St Michael and All Angels

Before the church was restored in 1855–56 there were the remains of a round-headed window in the N wall of the nave, above the arcade. This suggests that the core of the church was of 11th- or 12th-century date. Judging from the details of the N arcade, an aisle was added in the late 12th century; this,

General view from SE

Nave N arcade with painted Nativity (see also p. 68)

however, was taken down in 1774. During the Victorian restoration the aisle was reinstated, the chancel – which had been shortened – was also restored to its original dimensions, and the W tower rebuilt again, as it had been in 1603, with a new broach spire. The S aisle has a 13th-century arcade, and the chancel arch is of 1856. The E window is in the Decorated style, supposedly reconstructed in the 1850s on the basis of original fragments discovered in the churchyard. The S porch was rebuilt in 1683.

This eventful structural history was given a fresh impetus by the Second World War, during which an explosion shattered the stained glass of the body of the church; this was replaced by clear glazing, which is still in place. More positively, the interior of the church was painted out on the initiative of the then bishop of Chichester, Bishop Bell. The commission was given to the members of the Bloomsbury group, living at nearby Charleston, and carried out by Duncan Grant, Vanessa Bell and her son Quentin. Above the chancel arch is a striking Christ in Majesty by Grant; in the spandrels of the arch are clergy figures, including Bishop Bell, on the right, and representative servicemen on the left. On the N wall of the nave is the Adoration of the Shepherds, by Vanessa Bell, with her Annunciation on the S wall. The chancel walls were painted by Quentin. The pulpit was also painted, and two panels of the original scheme (showing archangels) survive, one by Vanessa, and one possibly by her daughter Angelica. The other panels were damaged in 1962 and repainted with flowers and fruit by Duncan Grant. The whole scheme has to be seen in the context of the same artists' painted decoration of Charleston Farmhouse, between Berwick and Firle, the colony's country retreat, which includes the furniture as well as the walls of the rooms.

Bishopstone, St Andrew

St Andrew's is an object lesson in reading a church fabric. It is built almost entirely of the basic Downland raw material – flint – with dressings (that is, quoins, window and door surrounds, and similar features) of sandstone blocks cut to shape. The running walling is at first sight homogeneous, but closer inspection shows that there are different ways of building using the same material. Looking at the church from the S, and reading from left to right, the W tower has flintwork built up in more or less horizontal courses (layers), each flint separated from the next, both horizontally and vertically, by a fair amount of mortar. Next come the nave and the S porch, where the flints are set randomly in the mortar matrix, with no apparent order, like the fruit in a Christmas cake. Some way to the right of the porch the fabric changes at the junction of the nave with the western element of the chancel (called 'choir' in the Buildings of England *East Sussex* volume) to a strictly, almost regimentally, coursed arrangement of the flints. The E wall of this part of the chancel and the narrower eastern element (called 'sanctuary') are built of random flints, but the distribution of the flints in the wall is much less dense than the random rubble of the nave and porch and the mortar matrix is a more noticeable feature of the fabric: blueberry muffin rather than rich fruit cake. The difference is immediately obvious looking from a point on the path just inside the lychgate.

So at least four different building episodes can be identified right away. The earliest of these appears to be the nave and porch. Fragmentary remains of the nave quoins suggest that it is Anglo-Saxon in date; not only is the SW quoin partly of the well-known 'long and short' variety, but there are similar remnants in the S wall at the junction of nave and 'choir' and high up in the W wall close to the N side of the tower. Original windows survive from this church in the N wall of the nave, visible from the N aisle, and in the S wall of the porch, where the outer reveal is blocked by the Anglo-Saxon sundial inscribed +EADRIC, reset from elsewhere in the building. The exact date of this early church is uncertain and has caused expert historians and archaeologists much head-scratching but,

Partly unblocked early window in S porch

Anglo-Saxon sundial

General view from E (further illustrations on pp. 23, 32 & 41)

on the basis of the remains of the quoins, is likely to be between AD950 and the end of the Anglo-Saxon period.

Next comes the tower, which covers two more original windows in the nave W wall, at some stage in the Norman period; it is deduced that it also covered the original W entrance to the church, and a new doorway had to be made in the S wall of the porch, where there had been none in the Anglo-Saxon period. This has scallop capitals and zigzag decoration typical of Romanesque architecture. There are similar details in the N arcade inside the 'choir', which must have replaced whatever chancel there had been in the Anglo-Saxon period, at about the same time as the present S door was added to the porch. The opening leading from the 'choir' to the 'sanctuary' is Romanesque, with multi-scalloped capitals on triple shafts, but the arch is pointed and has dog-tooth decoration, typical of the transition to the Gothic style, and to be dated 1180–1220. Inside the 'sanctuary', where the vaulting is of 1849, there are waterleaf capitals, which are consistent with this date.

The N aisle is clearly an addition to the original box-like nave: its W wall traps the surviving piece of NW quoin and one of its arcade arches cuts the Anglo-Saxon window mentioned above. The arcade's intermediate pier is circular with a round abacus above the capital; the arches are pointed and are slightly chamfered. The *Sussex: East* account suggests a date of *c*.1200, but finds this 'puzzling', because it assumes that the N aisle belongs to the same building campaign as the tower. But the fabric evidence does not support this assumption: the outer walls of the aisle are of the same 'blueberry muffin' variety of random flintwork as the 'sanctuary', which is of much the same date. In addition, the aisle windows, though they have semi-circular heads cut from single stone blocks, a Romanesque feature, also show a later detail: the angles between the openings and the wall plane are lightly chamfered, which is typical of the Transition. So the aisle was built at that popular time for such additions, the period around AD1200. Note that there is no range of clerestory windows, so the roof comes down in a single sweep from the ridge of the nave to the top of the low aisle wall – a so-called cat-slide roof, a type which is fairly common in SDNP.

Shortly after, in the 13th century, a new arch with stiff-leaf capitals was constructed between the nave and the 'choir', replacing whatever was there before – perhaps still the chancel arch of the Anglo-Saxon church. With that, the flurry of development, lasting at most 300 years, came to an abrupt end, as in so many Sussex churches, and St Andrew's settled down into its role of rural parish church. The historical evidence, which is complex and difficult to interpret, makes it clear that it must have been an important minster church in the pre-Conquest period, but like so many other minsters its original function as the mother church of an area beyond the immediate parish was superseded by the parochial organisation which had been developing in parallel, as it were, with the church fabric, and was also more or less complete by around 1200.

The 2006 renovation, which uncovered many details of the early church, revealed an area of paintwork on the nave W wall: though some chevron patterning can be discerned, no figurative content has been identified.

Ditchling, St Margaret's church

The church stands in a prominent position to the NW of the crossing point of the two routeways through the village and has a fairly extensive churchyard, which may originally have been larger to serve the surrounding area. There was a church here already in 1086 (DB) and before the Norman Conquest Ditchling was a royal estate, mentioned in

General view from SE (see also p. 16)

Alfred the Great's will and subsequently owned by Edward the Confessor. All this points to a church of great importance.

There are no obvious signs of the early Norman church, but it can be argued that the present nave survives from it: the style of the arches between the body of the church and the S aisle shows that it was built on about AD1200, so the nave must be earlier than that, i.e. in the Norman period. People have claimed to see some herringbone masonry in the W wall of the nave, which is often a sign of early date, but this seems to be wishful thinking. At all events, the nave is the earliest part of the fabric. Next came the long chancel in the 13th century, with pointed arches and colonnettes flanking the windows. What stood between the chancel and the nave is not known; possibly a small earlier chancel, perhaps a tower. At all events it was replaced by the present tower a little later in the 13th century. Then in the 14th a chapel was built to

Chancel interior facing NW

the S of the chancel (the Abergavenny Chapel, after the lords of the manor), and arches had to be cut in the chancel S wall to give access to it. This displaced the original S windows, and the shafts flanking them were reused around the typical Decorated tracery windows of the chapel.

The church and its surroundings benefited from the activities of the Guild of St Joseph and St Dominic and other artists and craftsmen who lived in Ditchling in the early 20th century, some of whom are buried in the churchyard. Eric Gill, perhaps the best known of them, contributed a grave surround and the sundial marking the coronation of King George V, while outside the churchyard is his Portland stone war memorial of 1920. One of his associates, Joseph Cribb, carved the screens around the Abergavenny Chapel in 1946 to the designs of John Denman, a local conservation architect responsible for restoring many Sussex churches.

Ditchling, Old Meeting house

Now the Unitarian Church, this was built in around 1730 as a General Baptist chapel. Like many Nonconformist places of worship of that period it is a brick structure and has a rather domestic appearance. The tall windows on the E front are a later addition. Inside there is a panelled timber gallery, also typical of the period – in Anglican churches as well – but the original underfloor baptistery for total immersion no longer exists. The chapel is surrounded by its own graveyard with an additional burial ground on the opposite side of the twitten (lane) leading from East End Lane (where the original entrance to the meeting house can still be seen) to Lewes Road (see illustrations on pp. 11 & 28).

East Dean and Jevington

East Dean, Sts Simon and Jude

At East Dean the tower stand to the N of the body of the church. This is not unexpected in a county that seems to specialise in lopsided plans, for example at Petworth and Stoughton (WSx), where the towers stand roughly midway along the S side. In the case of East Dean it is probable that the tower was built before the rest of the church, since it has features that point to a possible Anglo-Saxon date, especially the remains of the original S doorway with its 'megalithic' (large stone) jambs, visible inside the church, and the quoins on the S side, which extend down

to the ground, indicating that the tower was intended to stand free. It had its own W door, replaced in the 19th century, and to the E there was a semi-circular apse, revealed by excavation in 1979 and now marked out on the ground. There was an arch connecting this apse to the tower, which is visible inside the tower.

It appears, then, that the original church was tiny, consisting only of the space at the base of the tower, which served as a 'nave', and the apse. This is a known church type in the late Anglo-Saxon period, often referred to as a 'tower nave'. By coincidence, one might think, another of these tower naves survives at nearby Jevington, where it serves as the W tower of the later church. Once again, a quoin (at the NE angle) indicates the free-standing nature of the primary structure and the present arch into the nave originally led into a narrower structure – more likely a chancel than a nave. This arch is built of megalithic 'through stones', that is stones that

General view of East Dean from NW

East Dean, post-Reformation pulpit

Because of their small size these tower naves cannot have been intended for congregational use, but rather for worship by a small select group of people, most likely the residents of the local 'big house', so they were effectively private chapels. There is evidence at Jevington that this was the case: the church stands close to the manor house, and both are set in a roughly oval enclosure, so the status of the chapel seems to be assured. But there is no immediately obvious comparable evidence for East Dean.

In the post-Conquest period both churches expanded to make possible more inclusive public use. A regular nave and chancel were added to the S of the East Dean tower, but many of the features are later insertions and there are only a few traces of Romanesque detailing. In the E wall of the chancel are two shafts with shaft rings, which indicate that windows were put in in the 13th century. At the same date the S porch and the nave S door were added. The kingpost roof is 15th-century. The most significant addition to the building is the western extension with its small polygonal baptistery, designed by the firm of J L Denman, a Sussex architect, in 1961. Among the furnishings is the pulpit, dated 1623, complete with its back panel and sounding board – the 17th-century equivalent of a public address system.

Jevington, St Andrew

The nave and N aisle appear to be 13th-century, though they were heavily restored in 1873; the lancet windows in the chancel

Petrie's watercolour of Jevington from N, 1804 (note 'bedhead' memorial N of tower) (© Sussex Archaeological Society, Sharpe Collection no.191)

suggest a similar date, while the tower has a S doorway of slightly earlier date, c.1200. The furnishings include an ogee-headed 14th-century piscina, and a carved Caen stone slab of Saxo-Norman date in the N wall of the nave: the figure of Christ in a loincloth holds a staff with a cruciform head, at the foot of which is a small beast enmeshed in irregular interlace of Scandinavian type – a rarity in the south of the country. This presumably represents Christ triumphing over Evil, though the beast, and its smaller counterpart on the opposite side, looks rather tame and unthreatening.

In the chancel there is glass of the 1890s by Wimbledon Ladies' Art College, another rarity, but at least one other window of theirs exists in the church at Great Bookham, Surrey.

extend right across the sides of the opening or through the arch head, from one face of the wall to the other. This is another typical Anglo-Saxon technique.

(West) Firle, St Peter

There is no evidence here of an early church; the earliest survival is the N doorway, which is not *in situ*, with a semi-circular arch and two slight continuous chamfers, so around AD 1200. Apart from this, the chronology seems to start with the chancel in the 13th century, which has lancet windows and a trefoil headed piscina internally; of the same date the arch to the W tower and the S doorway, again not *in situ*. The side aisles appear to be of 14th-century date: the E windows have three lights with tracery in the Decorated style, but on the S side it was reset when the aisle was lengthened in the 15th century. Inside the aisle, a blocked opening in the NE corner is the former doorway to the rood loft stair. On the N side the E window may be in its original place, but that depends on whether the Gage Chapel was rebuilt in the 16th, as is often assumed; but the fabric of the gables suggests that it may have been just a remodelling of an existing chapel.

General view from SE

E end of S aisle showing blocked door to rood loft stair (further illustrations on pp. 60 & 72)

The nave arcades and the clerestory windows above have the appearance of 14th-century Decorated but are the result of a restoration in 1867, while the two-bay arcade into the Gage Chapel in the late Perpendicular style was added in 1884. The entrance to the chapel had previously been a doorway in the end wall of the N aisle, with a four-centred arch and foliate spandrels. Other architectural details of note include the late 16th-century crown-post roof and the stained glass: some late-medieval glass in the S aisle E window, a selection of 19th- and early 20th-century glass, and the highlight a Piper window of 1985 in the Gage Chapel E window, 'Homage to William Blake's Book of Job'.

St Peter's is best known, however, for the series of Gage family monuments. First there are the brasses: the earliest is to Bartholomew Bolney who died in 1476, and his wife: their daughter married into the Gage family; then there is Thomas Gage, d.1590, and another member of the family of about the same date. These are all at the E end of the N aisle. In the nave floor there is a brass to Mary Howard, d.1638, clad in a shroud. In the Gage Chapel are alabaster monuments made in 1595 by the Huguenot Garret Jansen (Johnson). They are the most important Elizabethan monuments in Sussex, in part because of the survival of the original drawings supplied by Jansen for approval by John Gage, d.1598, who commissioned the monuments; the running correspondence between the patron and the craftsman, in the form of comments and counter-comments written on the draft, is most revealing of the design process as well as serving to date the monuments themselves. The tomb chests bear effigies of those commemorated as well as brasses, inscriptions and heraldry, and are prime social history documents and a guide to fashionable dress at the end of the 16th century. The tomb of John Gage himself demonstrates the common practice of commissioning monuments in the lifetime of the patron.

Glynde, St Mary

This is an example, unique in Sussex and rare in the area of the Park as a whole, of a complete church newly built in a revived Classical style, and practically untouched since. It was begun in 1763 and completed in 1765, three years before building started at Avington (Hampshire), the closest comparison in SDNP, with which it has many features in common. Apart from quoins, base courses and the surrounds of openings, neither church employed the ashlar masonry frequently used in Classical buildings as a mark of sophistication; while Avington is built of brick, Glynde uses flint, but knapped to regular shapes rather than used whole. Both churches are effectively rectangular boxes without separate chancels; at Glynde there is a recess in the E wall which houses the altar reredos and allows the altar itself to obtrude only marginally into the body of the church. Above the reredos is a Venetian window, as there is at Avington.

Both buildings were funded by aristocratic patrons, in the case of Glynde the Right Reverend Dr Richard Trevor, Bishop of Durham, whose house, Glynde Place, stands only a few yards away from the church over the churchyard wall. This proximity reinforces the impression that St Mary's is more like a private chapel than a parish church. The bishop's patronage was recorded in the parish register of the time. The two-page entry includes a plan of old and new churches and concludes with an expression of thanks for

Interior looking down from W gallery (see also p. 10)

his Lordship's magnanimity, signed by the vicar and churchwardens. The plan shows that the old church was on a slightly different alignment from the new one, but comparable in size. It had a rectangular nave with a three-bay arcade through to a N aisle, a rectangular chancel, and a small S porch (see p. 10).

The new church lacks side aisles as well as a chancel; its windows are plain, with semi-circular heads. Externally there is a W porch with classical pediment bearing the Trevor arms in sculpted relief, and flanked by round-headed niches. In a domestic setting these would have been filled with figures from Classical antiquity or the busts of ancestors; in a Roman Catholic country they would have held images of saints; in the Protestant non-secular context they are left vacant (see p. 10).

Internally the furnishings and fittings are typical of their period. Congregational seating takes the form of high-backed, high-sided benches with doors ('box pews'), which provided a modicum of draught-free comfort during the lengthy sermons of the 18th century. Liturgical emphasis was on the Word of God, preached from the top level of what originally was a three-decker pulpit and proclaimed by 'lessons' from the Bible at reading desk level. The W gallery, which afforded extra seating, is also a typical feature of 18th-century interiors, but was in fact not built until 1841.

The coloured window glass is striking: it consists of 16th- and 17th-century Netherlandish panels reset between 1894 and 1916 in Renaissance-style surrounds by C E Kempe, the well-known local architect and designer.

Jevington – *see East Dean*

The town of Lewes

Lewes, the county town of East Sussex, is one of only two towns of any size totally within the confines of SDNP (the other is Petersfield, H). It has many places of worship that are worth visiting: several Anglican, one Roman Catholic, and an interesting crop of Nonconformist.

Slightly confusingly there are two churches dedicated to St John. To the N of the castle is *St John sub Castro*, traditionally the principal town church, though much of its parish lay outside the borough. It is thought to be the

Piddinghoe, circular W tower

South Malling, datestone in porch gable, 1628 (see also p. 27)

Lewes, St Anne: Petrie's watercolour of ?1803 showing site of anchoress's cell behind 'bedhead' memorial (© Sussex Archaeological Society, Sharpe Collection no.205)

successor of an Anglo-Saxon minster, and the present building of 1839–40 incorporates a doorway of late 11th-century design from the earlier church, which is shown in topographical drawings of the late 18th century. There is also an arch, possibly dating from about 1200, with an inscription in Lombardic characters referring to a Danish prince, Magnus, who lived here as an anchorite (hermit). *St John the Baptist* in Southover was fashioned out of the guest house at the N (main) gate of St Pancras' Priory, the principal Cluniac monastery in medieval England. This was systematically destroyed at the Dissolution, and its stone was used in part to build Southover Grange and is otherwise liberally distributed throughout Southover; architectural fragments also turn up frequently outside Lewes and are commonly attributed to the priory. St John's is perhaps best known for the black Tournai tomb slab for Gundrada, wife of the priory's founder, in the S chapel; it was carved posthumously probably a century after her death in 1085 (see p. 70). The remains of Gundrada and her husband were reinterred beneath the slab, having been discovered during excavation for the railway (which runs across the priory site) in lead cists decorated with rope moulding, now located in recesses in the chapel south wall.

All Saints', now a cultural centre, retains its late medieval W tower, but the body of the church was rebuilt in a Classical style in 1806–07 and still has its typical Georgian galleries on cast iron columns. On the High Street *St Michael's* has a round tower of the sort common in East Anglia, another area rich in chalk and flints; round towers are not common in Sussex but there are two others in the Ouse Valley, at Southease and Piddinghoe. Across the river from Lewes town centre is Cliffe, where *St Thomas à Becket* is a much-restored medieval church with a very early royal arms dated 1598. Also across the river is *St Michael's, South Malling*, built 1628–32 evidently on the site of a medieval collegiate church. This was associated with a deanery under the direct control of the archbishop of Canterbury; it was all demolished after the Dissolution, and the building may be another source of recycled stone, like St Pancras' Priory. Some of it, of course, was reused in St Michael's, principally in the W tower, but two small capitals of 13th-century date are reset either side of the E window.

At the top of the hill where Lewes High Street becomes Western Road, *St Anne's* is the one Lewes church with substantial *in situ* evidence from the Norman period, and is described in more detail below.

In the early modern period Lewes was a hotbed of political radicalism and religious Dissent, and it is no surprise to find Nonconformist places of worship well represented, though several are no longer used as such. Of interest are: the Unitarian *Westgate Chapel*, which developed out of a late 16th-century town house and exhibits a number of building periods; the *Friends' Meeting House* on Friars Walk, 1704 with an attached cottage in the Nonconformist tradition; *Jireh Chapel* of 1805 on Malling Street (Calvinistic Independent), timber-framed and covered with mathematical tiles, the interior with a dominant pulpit and clerk's desk and galleries on classical columns; and the *Baptist Church* on Eastgate Street, rebuilt in 1843 in a neo-Norman style – the Baptists stood out against the Gothic Revival styles longer than most.

St Anne's Church

The suburb of Westout lay outside the W gate of the borough of Lewes and spread up the hill as far as the E end of St Anne's church. Originally dedicated to St Mary, the church served a relatively small area and was subordinate to St Peter Westout, which was within the borough as extended in the Middle Ages. In 1539 St Peter's was abandoned and the two parishes amalgamated. From the mid-

17th century St Mary's was normally referred to as St Anne's, probably on account of the memory of a medieval cult of that saint; she is associated with wells and there is evidence for a well on the N side of Western Road, opposite the church.

[On the same side of the street there has been since 1870 the Roman Catholic *church of St Pancras*. It was rebuilt in 1938–39 by the son of F A Walters, who had been responsible for a number of well-designed churches for Roman Catholic parishes throughout Sussex, including Sacred Heart, Petworth (see above).]

Lewes, St Pancras (RC), with churchyard wall of St Anne's on left (further illustrations of St Anne's on pp. 34, 55, 76 & 125)

Returning to St Anne's, the evidence of the church fabric makes it clear that the basis of the building is a long narrow rectangle of the Norman period without side aisles but with a transept-like chapel on the S side. There are small round-headed windows in the E wall of the transept and the S wall of the nave, the

latter visible above the S arcade from the aisle. At the E end, the chancel was as wide as the nave, and there is no evidence for a chancel arch (the present one dates from 1889). At the W end is a tower, also with Romanesque windows and part of the first campaign of building.

In common with many other churches, St Anne's was extended sideways at the end of the 12th century: the arcade has circular piers with low square leaf-encrusted capitals above with pendant face masks below the projecting corners (this detail is also to be found nearby at Beddingham and Rodmell). The arches are pointed, heralding the transition to the Early English style and very plain, but with a slight chamfer instead of a sharp arris. The arch into the transept is still round-headed, however, but the transept itself was embellished by the insertion of a rib vault, which may indicate that an upper chamber was envisaged (but not a tower, since there already was one at the W end). However, this transept is the likely place for the altar to St Anne (before she became the patron saint), and this special covering of the chapel area may simply have been built in her honour.

In the following century the chancel was possibly lengthened; certainly the E wall and parts of the side walls were rebuilt. There is no evidence for this on the S side of the church, where much modern restoration has taken place, but a change in the masonry is visible on the N side to the left (E) of the middle window. Inside the chancel, corbels survive in the four corners, suggesting that a rib vault was intended, but it is not known whether the intention was ever carried out. In 1253 St Richard de Wych, bishop of Chichester, left in his will five shillings for the support of an anchoress (female hermit) in this church. The remains of her cell are preserved in the modern vestry: a hatch from the transept, through which food could be passed, a rudimentary seat, and two recesses, in one of which she was buried.

The furnishings of the church include the 18th-century W gallery with the arms of George IV below, part of the pulpit given in 1620, the probably original font with a carved basket-weave pattern, and amongst the glass there is continental work from 1889 by Capronnier of Brussels, who provided the glass for several churches, mainly in ESx, but only two of them (Offham and Westmeston) in SDNP.

Rodmell, St Peter

There are few clues to the chronology of the church building because of the extensive restorations carried out in the 19th century. Of the church recorded in Domesday Book there is no trace. The basis of the existing church appears to be 12th-century, but there is virtually nothing of this date visible on the exterior. Inside the chancel, however, is the reveal of a genuine window of the Norman period. It is heavily splayed and round-headed, but the narrow external opening has a pointed head, leading some commentators to suggest a 13th-century date. It is difficult to inspect this feature, which is now inside the modern vestry, but it is possible that its head has been retouched to make it look like an Early English lancet.

But accepting a date in the 12th century for the chancel, what of the rest of the church? Most accounts assume that the nave is of the

General view from E (see also p. 45)

same date, but there are no surviving period features to confirm this. However, there is a shred of evidence in the S aisle that allows a chain of reasoning leading to this conclusion. In the E wall of the aisle, beside the jamb of the arch into the SE chapel, is a short stretch of plinth – an external feature that indicates that the chapel was in existence before the building of the S aisle. Where in the chronology does the chapel fit? The present 14th-century arcade that separates it from the chancel, implying that the chapel is later, is in fact a rebuild. Slight evidence for an earlier arcade survives in the E respond: an impost at a lower level than the existing one, whose form is consistent with the date of the chancel. So the chapel is apparently an original feature.

Since the S aisle can be shown to be of later date, there must have been an aisle-less nave to which it was added in manner familiar from many other churches in SDNP. At that point the S arcade was inserted into the nave wall. It has semi-circular arches with a slight chamfer, supported on a round pier with a capital (stiff leaf: a 13th-century trait), which has corbel-like excrescences below the corners of the square abacus. One of them represents a human head. Similar capitals were used at Beddingham and at St Anne's in Lewes. This combination of features suggests a date around 1200, the classic period for the addition of side aisles, in the course of

Fragment of medieval glass from a Trinity scene

the Transition from Romanesque to Gothic. The end walls of the aisle have semi-circular arches to the SE chapel and the baptistery respectively, and their S responds appear to be genuine late 'Norman' work.

Also apparently of that period is the striking chancel arch, but this is a Victorian copy of an original with rich geometrical carving, said to have been made of stones brought from Lewes Priory, originally with a pointed arch. It must have been brought in in the 16th century. It includes shafts of black Tournai marble, a characteristic Priory material.

There is some fabric evidence externally for the continued development of the church. In the E wall of the chancel there is an important survival in the shape of the jambs and springings of earlier windows on either side of the existing Perpendicular E window. This implies a group of two or three separate windows with pointed heads, such as can be found for example at Piddinghoe or a triple window such as at South Malling. Also in the N wall of the chancel are traces of an earlier window above the 14th-century lowside. At the W end there is a tower with 13th-century windows and bell openings, and a baptistery on its S side with lancet windows. This must have followed shortly after the building of the S aisle. An arch with a pointed head was inserted in the W wall of the nave to give access to the tower; it was rather clumsily done. Finally, a change of fabric high up in the SE chapel wall shows that it was raised by several courses, presumably to allow the roof

pitch to be altered, at some unknown date; the new fabric returns for a short stretch along the E wall and stops abruptly at a vertical joint with the earlier walling, but the reason for this is not clear.

The church is not rich in furnishings and fittings: the font is square and of Purbeck type, with shallow blind arches. On the wall of the baptistery is hung part of a 14th-century timber screen. The most interesting medieval survival, however, is the small stained-glass Crucifixus of 15th-century date reset in one of the N windows. From the restorations of the 19th century there is paving of Minton tiles, an elaborate pulpit and a lectern that go with the reconstructed chancel arch, and glass of the 1850s and 1860s.

Westdean, All Saints

When viewed from the gate in the SW corner of the churchyard, the most striking thing about the church is the unusual W tower. It is as broad as the nave, whereas most W towers are square on plan and allow a view of the nave W wall. Here the impression is of a wide block of solid masonry, almost like a miniature continental *Westwerk*. The upper part of the tower was built upon an earlier substructure, either the W bay of the nave or a western extension to it. The same sort of thing happened at Sompting, but the Anglo-Saxon nave there was narrower than that at Westdean, and the resulting tower has the expected square plan. The evidence for the

General view from SW (further illustrations on pp. 44, 52 & 73)

structural development here is an offset in the S wall of the tower; the walling below is random flint rubble, and above is coursed flints. In the W wall the eye of faith can just make out the line of a gable beginning at the level of the corner buttresses, with its apex near the top of the later single-light window. This must indicate the height of the end wall of the original church.

There is no clear evidence in the tower fabric for its date, but assuming that it was integral with the present nave its chronology can be deduced from the surviving window at the W end of the N nave wall. This is a very simple single-light opening with jambs made of single stones and the head (originally semi-circular) cut from a single block. The date is probably

Chancel interior, N wall with medieval tomb recess interfering with splay of earlier window and Easter Sepulchre beyond; modern pulpit

late 11th- or early 12th-century. When the upper part of the tower was added in the 14th century the present finely carved arch was either inserted into an existing wall between tower and nave or constructed as part of a new dividing wall; the plaster on the interior walls means that it cannot be seen whether this wall is in bond with side walls or not.

The body of the church consists of a single long rectangular cell, with no division between the nave and the chancel. Most of the windows are 14th-century insertions, but there is evidence of 13th-century work at the E end. In the N chancel wall is a large lancet, partly obscured by the surround of a tomb recess of later 13th-century date. In the S wall, below the more easterly of the two windows, is the bottom half of a piscina recess, with filleted and hollow-chamfered mouldings and a projecting semi-circular bowl; its upper

parts were removed when the window was constructed, but what is left suggests that it was a very elegant feature.

The 14th century not only added these windows but also the one in the E wall with three traceried lights (flanked by 19th-century commandments boards), and a second tomb recess with crocketed gable and pinnacles typical of the Decorated style. It presumably served as the surround of an Easter Sepulchre. On the S side, between the windows, is a large standing wall monument to William Thomas (d.1639/40) and his wife Anne (d.1625): two alabaster figures flanked by columns and angels. On the N wall of the nave a tablet to Susan Tirrey (1637) with cherubs; in a recess in the S wall the bronze head of Oswald Birley (d.1952) and in the NW corner of the nave the bronze head of Lord Waverley (d.1958) by Jacob Epstein.

Willingdon, St Mary

The village has been all but swallowed up by Eastbourne, but a little of its original character survives around the church. St Mary's is full of intriguing puzzles and some really good monuments to members of the Parker family

Interior facing W showing gallery, organ case (in its 'correct' western position) and 15th-century crown-post roof

of nearby Ratton. First there is the position of the tower – both in the physical sense and in the sense of its place in the chronology of the building. Its position at the NW corner of the church is odd, but less so in the context of Sussex, a county that specialises in eccentrically-placed towers. What is odder is the cut-back roof weathering on its eastern face, which has been explained as evidence for an earlier church nave. But the problem is that the detail of the tower implies a date in the 13th century, while there are the remains of a window as early as this or even earlier in the S nave wall. The answer seems to be that the weathering belongs to an earlier version of the N aisle, which must have had a saddle-back roof; inside the church, on the N side of the nave wall, there are corbels which could have supported the southern slope of such a roof. All of this must have been of 13th-century date, and one is forced to conclude that the N arcade was rebuilt in the 14th, which has led previous commentators to assume that the aisle was of that date, too.

There is another weathering on the W wall of the nave, off-centre and with remains of a doorway below. This has been interpreted as the remains of a porch, but it would be unusual

W elevation of nave and NW tower (further illustrations on pp. 60 & 73)

for a main door into the church to be offset in this way. Other ideas have been put forward, but none is entirely satisfactory. Above this weathering and immediately above the string course at the SW corner is an inscribed stone, with the names of the churchwardens and the date 1650, when presumably some work was carried out on the gable end. The name Nicholas is written with a retrograde N and inverted As are used for the Us. Another inscription marks the addition of the brick angle buttresses to the tower in 1846.

At the E end of the church, the chancel dates from the 15th century, though the big E window with reticulated tracery is of the 19th. Also 15th-century is the impressive crown-post roof over the nave. The font is late-medieval, too, in the Perpendicular style, but its cover – and the W gallery – which are apparently in the style of Wren were made in 1953. In the following year Sir Ninian Comper added the rood at the entrance to the chancel.

There is a good range of glass, including one window by Comper; most colourful is the heraldic glass of 1622 (reset) in the N chapel E window, which depicts the various marriage alliances of the Parkers (the spouses' family names are mentioned in the window). The Parkers are also commemorated in the many monuments, both in the N chapel and elsewhere in the church. Against the N wall of the chapel is an architectural tablet with urn to Sir George, who died in 1726, and his wife Dame Mary. In the chancel another wall tablet to Sir John, d.1617, with a kneeling figure in alabaster. On the opposite wall an oval cartouche to Dame Katharine, née Parker, widow of Thomas Nutt: she died in 1700.

Further Reading

The first port of call to find out about those places of worship in SDNP necessarily omitted from this volume (and others) is the series of Pevsner Architectural Guides. Originally published in the Pelican Buildings of England series, *Sussex*, by Ian Nairn and Nikolaus Pevsner, appeared in 1965, and *Hampshire and the Isle of Wight*, by Nikolaus Pevsner and David Lloyd in 1967. Now published by Yale University Press, new editions have appeared for *Hampshire: Winchester and the North*, by Michael Bullen, John Crook, Rodney Hubbock and Nikolaus Pevsner (2010) and *Sussex: East with Brighton and Hove*, by Nicholas Antram and Nikolaus Pevsner (2013). Revised editions for southern Hampshire and West Sussex are in preparation.

An *Architectural & Historic Review of Churches in the Roman Catholic Diocese of Arundel and Brighton*, by Teresa Sladen and Nicholas Antram, appeared in 2005. Nonconformist places of worship are described in the *Inventory of Nonconformist Chapels and Meeting-houses*, by Christopher Stell and published by the former Royal Commission for the Historical Monuments of England: Hampshire chapels in the volume for South-West England (1991)

and Sussex chapels in the Eastern England volume (2002). Sussex is also covered by *Sussex Churches and Chapels*, by David Beevers, Richard Marks and John Roles (Brighton Pavilion, Art Gallery and Museums 1989).

There is a wealth of literature on English parish churches and their furnishings and monuments; much was published in the early years of the 20th century and is now available only in libraries and antiquarian bookshops; the Rev Dr J C Cox and Francis Bond were prolific authors. Among more recent books are *Churches in the Landscape,* by Richard Morris (1989 and later editions), *Church Furnishing and Decoration in England and Wales*, by Gerald Randall (Batsford 1980), *English Church Monuments*, by Brian Kemp (Batsford 1980), and the more specialist *East Sussex Church Monuments, 1530-1830*, by Nigel Llewellyn (Sussex Record Society 2011). On mural decoration there are *Medieval Wall Paintings*, by Clive Rouse (Shire 1991) and *Medieval Wall Paintings in English & Welsh Churches*, by Roger Rosewell (Boydell Press 2008).

For further information on how to study a church building there are *Churches and*

Chapels: investigating Places of Worship, by David Parsons (2nd edition, CBA 1998) and *The Archaeology of Churches*, by Warwick Rodwell (Amberley 2012).

Topographical drawings can be a valuable source of information, particularly about medieval churches replaced or heavily rebuilt in the 19th century. In the late 18th century S H Grimm and the James Lamberts drew a great number of churches, and in the early to mid-19th Henry Petrie in Sussex and Richard Ubsdell in Hampshire produced many watercolours and line drawings of churches. The originals are variously kept by the British Library, the Sussex Archaeological Society, Portsmouth Museum and Records Service and Winchester Cathedral, and many have been reproduced in books and catalogues and on line.

Online resources include the excellent website http://www.sussexparishchurches.org. The records of the Incorporated Church Building Society, which are valuable for studying the restorations of the 19th century, are available on the Lambeth Palace Library site: http://images.lambethpalacelibrary.org.uk/luna/servlet/LPLIBLPL~34~34

Glossary

Abacus – Flat slab at the top of a capital

Aisle – Area flanking and parallel to one of the main spaces of a church (nave or chancel)

Alabaster – A soft, easily carved stone from the area around Derbyshire/Staffordshire, frequently used for tombs and effigies

Apse – Semi-circular or polygonal end to a compartment, especially a chancel

Arcade – A continuous row of two or more arches

Arris roll – A cylindrical-shaped moulding at the junction of two surfaces at right angles to each other

Baluster – A colonnette or spindle of bellying form, often as a handrail support

Billet – Ornament formed of small rectangular blocks, often applied in two or more rows in alternating positions

Blind – A term applied to features on the surface of a wall without any aperture

Box pews – Seating enclosed with panelling and entered by a small door

Broach spire – An octagonal spire mounted on a square tower, where the spaces between the non-cardinal faces and the corner of the tower are covered by pyramidal blocks of stone

Cable moulding – Longitudinal shaped stone or timber with the appearance of twisted strands of rope

Capital – A block of stone at the head of a column or pier carrying the masonry above

Chamfer – A diagonal edge or corner

Chancel – A compartment to the east of the nave or central tower of a church

Chantry – An endowment providing for a priest or priests to sing Masses for specified persons or institutions

Clerestory (clearstory) – The upper walling of a main compartment, normally above the roof level of an adjoining aisle, and provided with windows

Coffering – An arrangement of sunken panels decorating a ceiling or the underside of a vault or arch

College – A body of priests (not monks) attached to a church

Commandments board – A panel or panels with the painted texts of the Ten Commandments, the Lord's Prayer and the Creed

Communion rail – A low balustrade enclosing the altar-space in a chancel or chapel

Corbel – A stone projecting from the wall supporting something above, e.g. a vertical roof timber

Course – A continuous horizontal layer of stones

Coursed – Masonry in which the stones are laid in horizontal courses

Crocket – A carved projection from an architectural feature – arch, pinnacle, spire – as part of the embellishment of its external face; typical of the Decorated style

Crossing – The space in the centre of a cruciform church, usually below the (crossing) tower

Cruciform – A church whose plan is in the form of a cross, usually with a tower at the centre of four radiating limbs – chancel, transepts, nave

Cusp – Points of stone projecting into the spaces formed by the stone bars of window tracery, giving the space a 'frilly' or 'foiled' shape (see Quatrefoil below)

Decorated – The sub-style of Gothic architecture current in the first half of the 14th century, characterized by the use of the ogee arch (see below)

Dissent – Protestant protest against the hierarchy and liturgy of the established Church of England, which was held not to have distanced itself sufficiently from the norms of the Roman Catholic Church; it led to secession and the formation of Nonconformist groups, such as Congregationalists, Baptists, etc.

Doom – In the late Middle Ages, the depiction of the Last Judgement painted on the east wall of the nave, above the chancel arch

Dressed stone – Stone which has been deliberately shaped by a mason

Early English – The sub-style of Gothic architecture current in the late 12th and 13th centuries, characterized by the use of the sharply pointed arches and dogtooth ornament

Easter sepulchre –A recess in the north wall of the chancel, near the altar; for more detail see the description in the section on Furnishings and Fittings

Flèche – A spirelet

Fresco – Mural painting in which pigment is applied to new plaster before it has dried

Geometric – A development of the Early English style of Gothic architecture current in the second half of the 13th century, characterized by the use of geometrical forms, especially circles, in window tracery

Gothic – The later medieval style of architecture, which succeeded Romanesque after a period of Transition in the late 12th century and continued until the mid-16th century, with later revivals

Gothick – A version of neo-Gothic current in the late 18th and early 19th centuries, which was guided more by inspiration than by close observation of the genuine Gothic styles

Graffito – Scratched decoration or lettering on plaster or dressed stone surfaces

Hipped gable – A gable which is not a vertical continuation of the end wall beneath it, but part of the roof structure which slopes backward towards the ridge of the roof

Hood mould – A projecting stone moulding around the head of an opening

Hundred – The traditional subdivision of a county, originally conceived as an area of 100 hides (a hide supposedly could support one family)

Impasto – In painting, colour laid on thickly

Impost – A horizontal moulding between the jamb and the springing (beginning) of the arch which it supports

Indent – (A stone slab with) a shallow chiselled recess to take a memorial brass plate, so that it lies flush with the surface of the stone

Jamb – The vertical side support of an opening

Lancet – A narrow single-light window with a sharply pointed head

Liturgy – A set form of church service, which may be written down (Roman Missal, Book of Common Prayer) or simply an informal tradition (as practised by some Nonconformist groups)

Lowside (window) – A generally small window in a chancel wall, usually towards the west end and most frequently found on the south side; lowsides are normally at a lower level than the rest of the chancel fenestration

Minster – In the early Middle Ages a church serving a 'territory' larger than the later parish, and having a staff of priests

Moulding – A projecting linear feature in stone carved to a simple or elaborate shape in cross-section

Mullion – A vertical stone divider between the lights of a window of two or more vertical subdivisions

Nave – The body of a church for congregational use

Oculus – A circular window

Offset – A horizontal level at which the vertical wall plane steps back; sometimes marked by a string course (see below)

Ogee – A curved arch or moulding in which the curve changes direction, forming a shape like an elongated letter S

Pediment – A low gable-shaped feature used as a form of decoration or as part of a Classical architectural feature

Perpendicular – The sub-style of Gothic architecture current from the mid-14th century until the mid-16th, characterized by elaborate panel work based on vertical straight lines, either as window tracery or as wall decoration

Pier – An arch support built of individual stones or bricks, rather than the complete round drums of stone that make up a column

Pilaster strip – A projecting strip of dressed stone rising vertically through a (usually rubble) wall, characteristic of the late Anglo-Saxon style

Piscina – A basin with a drain hole for the reception of ablution water at the Mass; usually a recess in the wall to the south of a medieval altar, but some early examples survive from the 12th century of free-standing pillar piscinas

Porticus – Side chambers attached to Anglo-Saxon church buildings, entered from the body of the church; not porches, but note the south porticus at Bishopstone (ESx), later converted into a porch by the insertion of a Romanesque doorway

Purgatory – A concept finally formulated by the Western (Roman Catholic) Church in the 13th century whereby human souls were held to spend a transition period between death and Judgement, at which they would be assigned to Heaven or Hell; Purgatory afforded the opportunity of atonement for sins

Quatrefoil –A four-lobed shape achieved by adding cusps (see above) to a circle; similarly trefoil (three lobes), cinquefoil (five lobes), which can also be added to an arch head

Quoin –A corner (French *coin*) usually of dressed stones set in a systematic pattern

Random – Not coursed

Reredos – A painted or sculpted background to an altar

Respond – A half-pier at the end of an arcade supporting the last arch

Reveal – The inner opening of a door or window

Roll moulding – A cylindrical-shaped linear moulding

Romanesque – The style of architecture current in the 11th and 12th centuries, characterized by semi-circular arches and geometrically-shaped capitals; formerly known as 'Norman' in the British Isles

Rood – The great composition consisting of a crucifix and flanking figure of St Mary and St John mounted above the entry into the chancel

Rood loft – A gallery across the church at the foot of the rood; see also the *Selected Churches* entry for Easton (H)

Rood screen – The screen across the chancel arch merging into the rood loft above

Rubble – Undressed stone

Scallop – A cone-shaped moulding often used on Romanesque capitals

Secco – Mural painting applied to dry plaster

Sedilia – Clergy seats in the chancel in the form of recesses in the south wall

Spandrel – A sub-triangular area between an arch and the surrounding frame of a doorcase or between two arches of an arcade

Splay – The widening of a window from a narrow aperture to a broader one

String course – A horizontal course or moulding projecting from the surface of a wall

Tester – A sounding board above a pulpit

Three- (two-) decker pulpit – A pulpit on several levels incorporating the preaching rostrum, a lectern, and a clerk's desk; see also the *Selected Churches* entry for Avington (H).

Tower-church – A church in which the bottom stage of the tower serves as the nave of the church

Tracery – A pattern of shaped stone mouldings in a window arch

Transept – A side chamber at right angles to the axis of a church

Transition/al – Refers to the period (late 12th and early 13th centuries) between the Romanesque and Gothic styles when features of both styles were used together in various combinations

Transom – A horizontal window bar

Vault – An arched stone roof or ceiling

Waterleaf – A type of leaf, broad and flat with a curled tip, used in the decoration of capitals in late Romanesque and Transitional buildings

Acknowledgements

The authors are indebted to Portsmouth Museum Service for the illustrations of Clanfield and Petersfield, to the Dean and Chapter of Winchester for the illustration of Privett, and to the Sussex Archaeological Society for Henry Petrie's drawings from the Sharpe Collection; to Roger Wilmshurst for the photographs of Coombes, to Roger Rosewell for those of Poynings, to David Boys for Hardham, to Lisa Fisher for West Chiltington, and to Kevin Newman for Washington; to Jo Bartholomew and David Rymill of Winchester Cathedral for advice on the Privett illustration; to Charles O'Brien (Pevsner Architectural Guides) and Yale University Press for kindly sharing information on East Hampshire churches; to Dr John Crook and Christopher Whittick for help and advice; to Dr John Manley for managing the editorial processes and Jan Newbury for proof-reading. Above all, we wish to thank Professor Eric Fernie for generously offering us valuable advice.

Index of Places

(italicised numerals indicate pages on which there are illustrations)